BEGINNER'S GUIDE TO
CAKE DECORATING

BEGINNER'S GUIDE TO
CAKE DECORATING

First edition published in 2011

LOVE FOOD is an imprint of Parragon Books Ltd

Parragon
Queen Street House
4 Queen Street
Bath BA1 1HE, UK

Copyright © Parragon Books Ltd 2011

LOVE FOOD and the accompanying heart device is a registered trade mark of Parragon Books Ltd in Australia, the UK, USA, India, and the EU.

www.parragon.com

ISBN: 978-1-4454-2296-1

Printed in China

Author and home economist: Joanna Farrow
Photographer: Sian Irvine

Notes for the Reader
This book uses imperial, metric, and US cup measurements. Follow the same units of measurement throughout; do not mix imperial and metric. All spoon measurements are level: teaspoons are assumed to be 5 ml, and tablespoons are assumed to be 15 ml. Unless otherwise stated, milk is assumed to be whole, eggs are large, individual vegetables, such as potatoes, are medium, and pepper is freshly ground black pepper.

The times given are an approximate guide only. Preparation times differ according to the techniques used by different people and the cooking times may also vary from those given as a result of the type of oven used. Optional ingredients, variations or serving suggestions have not been included in the calculations.

Recipes using raw or very lightly cooked eggs should be avoided by infants, the elderly, pregnant women, convalescents, and anyone with a chronic condition. Pregnant and breastfeeding women are advised to avoid eating peanuts and peanut products. People with nut allergies should be aware that some of the ready-prepared ingredients used in the recipes in this book may contain nuts. Always check the packaging before use.

Contents

Introduction

EQUIPMENT

Most of the recipes in this book require minimal equipment, some of which you might already have. However, some specialty items are worthwhile investments, making techniques easier and improving your skills. Cake decorating shops and good kitchenware stores are useful sources, or check the many Internet suppliers.

Baking Equipment

✳ Cake Pans
Strong, sturdy, deep cake pans can be expensive but will last a lifetime. The most useful sizes for a simple birthday or Christmas cake are 8–9-inch/ 20–23-cm round pans or 7–8-inch/ 18–20-cm square pans; tiered cakes for weddings and other special occasions require two to three pan sizes. Choose pans that are at least 3¼ inches/8 cm

deep so that deep cakes do not spill over the sides. Rent pans if you plan to use them only once. Other useful pans include a 12-section cupcake pan, loose-bottom round and square cake pans, and a fluted Bundt pan.

✳ Paper Cupcake Liners
These are available in many different colors, patterns, and sizes. The

recipes in this book use liners that measure 2 inches/5 cm across the bottom and 1½ inches/4 cm deep. Cupcake liners do not need greasing.

✳ Electric Mixers
These make it much easier to mix cake ingredients and frostings. Handheld ones are easy to manage or, for large cakes, a freestanding mixer is ideal. The same results can be achieved by beating the batter with a wooden spoon or balloon whisk, but it will take longer.

✳ Mixing Bowls
An assortment of sizes is useful. Glass bowls are good for softening butter in the microwave before adding the other ingredients.

✳ Measuring Spoons
These are good for accurately measuring small amounts of ingredients, such as baking powder, baking soda, and cake flavorings.

✳ Measuring Cups
A standard set of kitchen measuring cups come in ¼, ⅓, ½, and 1 cup sizes. Make sure dry ingredients are level by using the top edge of a knife to remove any excess. A glass measuring cup is also essential for measuring liquids.

✳ Wax and Parchment Paper
These can be interchangeable. Wax paper is used for lining pans. Parchment paper is stronger, making it ideal for making pastry bags (see page 9) and for placing decorations on.

Lining a Round Cake Pan: Place the pan on a sheet of wax paper, draw around it, and cut out.

Cut a strip of paper at least 1¼ inches/3 cm deeper than the pan and make a ½-inch/1-cm fold along one long edge. Snip the folded edge at ¾-inch/2-cm intervals.

Grease the pan with melted butter and position the paper strip so the folded edge sits on the bottom. Cut and fit more strips to line the sides completely. Fit the circle of paper into the bottom. Grease the paper.

Lining a Square Cake Pan: Use the same technique as for lining a round cake pan—place the pan on a sheet of wax paper, draw around it, and cut out. Cut a strip of paper at least 1¼ inches/3 cm deeper than the pan, and make a ½-inch/1-cm fold along one long edge. However, this time snip the folded edge only at the corners so the paper fits squarely into the corners of the pan.

Lining Layer Cake Pans: Grease the pans and line the bottoms with circles or squares of wax paper. Dust the greased sides of the pans with flour, tapping out the excess.

✳ **Pastry Brush**
A good pastry brush is useful for greasing pans and brushing cakes with glaze before decorating.

✳ **Kitchen Scissors**
Scissors are needed for cutting paper for lining pans, snipping tips off pastry bags, and cutting ribbons and other decorations.

✳ **Sifters and Strainers**
A sifter is useful for sifting flour and confectioners' sugar that might have caked together in the package during storage. A small, fine strainer or tea strainer is useful for dusting confectioners' sugar over a cake.

✳ **Spatulas**
Flexible plastic spatulas are used for beating cake mixtures and frostings together and for ensuring there is no wastage when scraping out mixes from bowls.

✳ **Wire Cooling Rack**
Most cakes are cooled on wire racks so air can circulate and cool them quickly. Cakes with a higher sugar content, such as a rich fruitcake or chocolate cake, are usually cooled completely in the pan.

Decorating Equipment

✱ Cake Boards
Cake boards that are ½-inch/1-cm deep are sometimes referred to as "drums." Available in round, square, heart, and other shapes, cake boards come in various types of material strong enough to take any size cake. Cake boards can be used for separating tiers when stacking a cake.

✱ Toothpicks
These are useful for dotting tiny amounts of food coloring into icing and for easing toppings or melted chocolate into corners.

✱ Fondant Smoother
This is a flat plastic tool that creates a perfectly smooth surface when applying ready-to-use fondant. These are available in two different styles: a general-purpose one for both the top and sides of a cake and one specifically for smoothing the sides of a cake.

✱ Rolling Pin
A large wooden rolling pin can be used for all aspects of cake decorating, from applying marzipan to rolling fondants and decorations. Stainless steel, ceramic, or plastic ones are less likely to damage the toppings and are available in small sizes, perfect for rolling intricate decorations.

✱ Knives
Use a small, sharp kitchen knife for trimming marzipan and icing. An artist's knife is better for cutting out intricate decoration shapes and around templates.

✱ Palette Knife
Choose a good-quality, flexible knife for spreading preserves, buttercream, and various frostings.

✱ Paintbrushes
A very fine-tipped brush is useful for painting fine lines and decorations. A larger brush is good for moistening surfaces and dusting.

✱ Metal and Plastic Cutters
These are available in many different shapes and sizes, from basic round cutters to intricate flower shapes, numbers, and letters.

✳ Turntable
Resting a cake, on its board or plate, on a turntable enables you to turn the cake very easily as you decorate.

✳ Ruler
Use a metal or plastic ruler for making pastry bags, measuring pan and cutter sizes, and accurately gauging spaces between decorations.

✳ Plastic Dowels
Dowels are used to support the tiers of a stacked wedding or celebration cake.

✳ Tweezers
A small pair of tweezers is useful for positioning small decorations, such as silver balls.

✳ Wallpaper Scraper
These can be used for making chocolate caraque (see page 42). Keep one specifically for this purpose.

✳ Pastry Bags
These are easy to make from parchment paper and can also be bought as disposable bags or reusable nylon bags. To make a paper pastry bag, cut out a 10-inch/ 25-cm square from parchment paper and fold the paper diagonally in half to make a triangle. Cut the paper in half, just to one side of the folded line, to make two triangles. Hold one triangle with the long edge away from you and curl the right point over to meet the central point, forming a cone shape. Curl the left point over the cone so the three points meet. Adjust the points, if necessary, so there is no hole at the tip of the cone. Fold the points over to secure the cone in place.

✳ Piping Tips
Nozzles are available in a wide range of sizes and designs. Large tips are used for piping generous swirls of buttercream or frosting onto cupcakes. Smaller tips are used for piping stars, lines, dots, or writing. The recipes in this book use a large star tip, ½ inch/1 cm across the tip, a smaller ¼-inch/5-mm star nozzle, and a fine writer nozzle.

BASIC CAKE RECIPES

Rich Chocolate Cake

This cake is rich, moist, and easy to slice. Once cool, wrap in foil and store in a cool place for up to three days or freeze. Unwrap and let stand overnight to defrost before decorating.

Round pan	4-inch/10-cm	6-inch/15-cm	8-inch/20-cm	10-inch/25-cm
Square pan	3¼-inch/8-cm	5-inch/13-cm	7-inch/18-cm	9-inch/23-cm
Unsweetened cocoa	¼ cup	½ cup	1 cup	1¾ cups
Boiling water	½ cup	1 cup	1¼ cups	2⅓ cups
Semisweet chocolate, chopped	2½ oz/70 g	4½ oz/125 g	9 oz/250 g	14 oz/400 g
Butter, softened	4 tbsp	½ cup	1 cup	1½ cups
Light brown sugar, packed	½ cup	1 cup	2¼ cups	3⅓ cups
Eggs, beaten	1	2	4	6
All-purpose flour	¾ cup	1⅓ cups	3 cups	4⅓ cups
Baking soda	½ tsp	½ tsp	¾ tsp	1½ tsp
Vanilla extract	1 tsp	2 tsp	4 tsp	2 tbsp
Baking time at 325°F (160°C)	**1 hour**	**1½ hours**	**2 hours**	**2¾ hours**
Serves	**4**	**10**	**20**	**30**

1. Preheat the oven to 325°F/160°C. Grease and line the required cake pan (see page 7). Put the cocoa in a heatproof bowl and gradually whisk in the boiling water until smooth. Immediately add the chocolate and let cool, stirring the mixture frequently until the chocolate melts.

2. Put the butter and sugar in a large mixing bowl and beat with an electric mixer to soften. Add the eggs, flour, baking soda, and vanilla and beat until combined. Stir in the chocolate mixture until evenly mixed. Spoon into the prepared pan and smooth the surface.

3. Bake in the preheated oven for the time stated in the chart above, or until firm to the touch and a toothpick inserted into the center comes out nearly clean. Let cool in the pan.

Vanilla Layer Cake

This is a moist, buttery yellow cake. It can be stored in an airtight container for 1–2 days before decorating, but should be frozen if keeping for longer. Defrost overnight before decorating. These cakes can be sandwiched with buttercream (and preserve, if desired), cream cheese frosting, or chocolate ganache before decorating.

Two round layer cake pans	4-inch/10-cm	6-inch/15-cm	8-inch/20-cm	10-inch/25-cm
Two square cake pans	*	*	7-inch/18-cm	9-inch/23-cm
Butter, softened	4½ tbsp	½ cup	1¼ cups	2¼ cups
Superfine sugar	⅓ cup	½ cup	1⅓ cups	2½ cups
Eggs, beaten	1	2	5	9
Vanilla extract	½ tsp	1 tsp	1 tbsp	2 tbsp
Self-rising flour	½ cup	1 cup	2¼ cups	4 cups
Milk	2 tsp	1½ tbsp	3 tbsp	5 tbsp
Baking time at 350°F (180°C)	15 minutes	25 minutes	35–40 minutes	45–50 minutes
Serves	4	8	16	26

*Square cake pans are not available in these sizes. To make yellow layer cakes in these sizes, use deep cake pans and bake half of the mixture at a time.

1. Preheat the oven to 350°F/180°C. Grease and line the required pans (see page 7). Put the butter and sugar into a mixing bowl and beat together with an electric mixer until creamy and very pale.

2. Gradually beat in the eggs, adding a little at a time so the mixture doesn't start to separate. If it does, beat in a little of the flour. Stir in the vanilla extract.

3. Sift the flour into the bowl and stir in gently with a large metal spoon. Stir in the milk. Divide between the prepared cake pans and smooth the surfaces. Bake in the preheated oven for the time stated above, or until the surface feels just firm to the touch.

4. Loosen the edges of the cakes with a knife and turn out onto a wire rack to cool.

Flavor Variations
For each egg in the quantity chart above, add the following ingredients (beating in after the eggs):
Lemon—finely grated zest of ½ lemon, plus lemon juice to replace the milk.
Orange—finely grated zest of ¼ orange, plus orange juice to replace the milk.
Almond—add ¼ tsp almond extract and substitute 2 tbsp of flour with 2 tbsp of ground almonds.

Vanilla Cupcakes

MAKES 12

◆ Preparation time:
10 minutes

◆ Cooking time:
20–25 minutes

INGREDIENTS

✱ ¾ cup butter, softened

✱ ¾ cup superfine sugar

✱ 3 eggs

✱ 1¼ cups self-rising flour

✱ 2 tsp vanilla extract

✱ 1 tbsp milk

Cupcakes are the easiest to make of all cakes. There is no greasing or lining of pans and the batter is mixed together in one easy stage. Paper liners and silicone cups come in an interesting range of colors and designs, so choose ones that suit your decorations or party theme. For sizes, see page 6.

1. Preheat the oven to 350°F/180°C. Line a 12-section cupcake pan with paper liners. Put all of the ingredients in a mixing bowl and beat with an electric mixer for 1–2 minutes, until the batter is smooth and creamy.

2. Divide the batter among the liners, making sure you fill each liner fairly evenly and fill each liner only three-quarters full. Bake in the preheated oven for 20–25 minutes, or until the surface feels just firm to the touch. Transfer to wire racks to cool.

For chocolate cupcakes: substitute ¼ cup of the flour with ¼ cup of unsweetened cocoa.

Carrot Cake

SERVES 12–14

◆ Preparation time:
25 minutes

◆ Cooking time:
30–40 minutes

INGREDIENTS

✱ ¾ cup butter, softened

✱ 1 cup packed light brown sugar

✱ 3 eggs, beaten

✱ 1¾ cups self-rising flour

✱ 2 tsp baking powder

✱ ½ tsp baking soda

✱ 1½ tsp ground cinnamon

✱ 1 cup ground almonds

✱ ⅓ cup golden raisins

✱ 3 carrots, finely grated

✱ ⅔ cup finely chopped fresh pineapple

This is a deliciously moist cake, perfect for any occasion, from an afternoon snack to a special birthday. It will keep fresh in an airtight container for a couple of days, but it is better to freeze it, if you want to store it for longer. Once decorated, it will keep fresh in a cool place for up to 5 days.

1. Preheat the oven to 350°F/180°C. Grease and line two 8-inch/20-cm layer cake pans (see page 7), each at least 1½ inches/4 cm deep.

2. Put the butter and sugar into a mixing bowl and beat with an electric mixer until smooth and creamy. Gradually beat in the eggs, adding a little at a time so the mixture doesn't start to separate. If it does, beat in a little of the flour.

3. Sift the flour, baking powder, baking soda, and cinnamon into the bowl and stir in gently with a large metal spoon. Add the almonds, golden raisins, carrots, and pineapple and stir

in until evenly combined. Divide equally between the pans and smooth the surface.

4. Bake in the preheated oven for 30–40 minutes, or until risen and just firm to the touch. A toothpick inserted into the centers of the cakes should come out clean. Let cool in the pans for 10 minutes, then transfer to a wire rack to cool.

Rich Fruitcake

Once cooked and cooled, fruitcake should be wrapped in wax paper and a double thickness of foil. Store the cake in a cool, dry place for 1–3 months. Before storing, if desired, unwrap and pierce the cake all over with a skewer and drizzle with 2–4 tablespoons of additional liqueur (depending on the size of the cake). Rewrap and repeat during the storage period, as desired. Rich fruitcake is also delicious served freshly baked, although it is less easy to slice.

Round pan	4-inch/10-cm	6-inch/15-cm	8-inch/20-cm	10-inch/25-cm
Square pan	3¼-inch/8-cm	5-inch/13-cm	7-inch/18-cm	9-inch/23-cm
Mixed dried fruit	1½ cups	3½ cups	5 cups	10 cups
Brandy, sherry, or orange juice	2 tbsp	4 tbsp	½ cup	⅔ cup
Butter, softened	4 tbsp	½ cup	1 cup	2 cups
Dark brown sugar, packed	¼ cup	½ cup	1 cup	2 cups
Eggs, beaten	1	2	5	9
All-purpose flour	⅔ cup	1⅔ cups	2¾ cups	4⅓ cups
Ground allspice	1 tsp	2 tsp	5 tsp	2 tbsp
Molasses	2 tsp	1 tbsp	2 tbsp	4 tbsp
Natural candied cherries, halved	3 tbsp	¼ cup	½ cup	1 cup
Blanched almonds, chopped	¼ cup	⅓ cup	¾ cup	1⅓ cups
Baking time at 275°F (140°C)	1¼–1½ hours	2¼–2½ hours	3¼–3½ hours	4–4¼ hours
Serves	6	16	30	50

1. Grease and line the required cake pan (see page 7). Put the mixed dried fruit into a mixing bowl and stir in the liqueur or juice. Cover and let stand for several hours or overnight, until the liquid has been absorbed, stirring once or twice.

2. Preheat the oven to 275°F/140°C. Put the butter and sugar in a mixing bowl and beat with an electric mixer until pale and creamy. Gradually add the beaten eggs, beating well after each addition. Add a little of the flour if the mixture starts to separate.

3. Sift the flour and spice into the bowl and stir in until combined. Stir in the molasses, then the steeped fruit and any unabsorbed liqueur, plus the cherries and almonds.

4. Spoon into the prepared pan and smooth the surface. Tie a double thickness of brown paper around the outside of the cake pan (this prevents the edges of the cake from overcooking before the center is cooked through). Bake in the preheated oven for the time stated above, or until a toothpick inserted into the center comes out clean. Let stand to cool in the pan.

FROSTINGS AND ICINGS

The frostings and icings on these two pages are those most frequently used in this book. See individual recipes for how to use and store.

MAKES 1 QUANTITY

✦ Preparation time:
5 minutes

INGREDIENTS
* ½ cup unsalted butter, softened
* 1¼ cups confectioners' sugar
* 1 tbsp hot water

Buttercream

This simple buttercream can be spread with a palette knife or is easy to pipe, both in fine lines or generous swirls. Store in the refrigerator in a sealed container for up to a week and let come to room temperature before use.

1. Put the butter in a mixing bowl and beat with an electric mixer to soften. Add the sugar and beat well until smooth and creamy.

2. Add the hot water and beat again until very soft and fluffy in texture.

Flavor Variations
Lemon—use 2 tbsp lemon juice instead of the water and add the finely grated rind of 1 lemon.
Orange—use 2 tbsp orange juice instead of the water. Add finely grated rind of 1 small orange.
Chocolate—blend ¼ cup unsweetened cocoa with 2 tbsp boiling water to make a paste. Add

to the buttercream with 2 tsp vanilla extract and beat until smooth and creamy.

Covering Cakes with Buttercream
Cakes can be spread with buttercream as a decoration or prior to covering with ready-to-use fondant. If using as a decoration, spread thinly with a palette knife, chill for 15 minutes to seal in the crumbs, then spread with a thicker, even layer of buttercream. Add texture by tilting the palette knife at an angle to create ridges or spread smoothly by holding the palette knife flat.

MAKES 1 QUANTITY

✦ Preparation time:
10 minutes

INGREDIENTS
* ½ cup cream cheese
* 3½ tbsp unsalted butter, softened
* 1 tsp lemon juice
* ¾ cup confectioners' sugar

Cream Cheese Frosting

This is traditionally used as a filling and covering for carrot cake but is also delicious with chocolate cake or vanilla yellow cake. It is easy to spread and pipe and keeps for a few days in the refrigerator before use. Cakes decorated with this frosting are best eaten within two days.

1. Beat together the cream cheese and butter with an electric mixer until smooth.

2. Add the lemon juice and confectioners' sugar and beat again until the frosting is light and creamy.

Royal Icing

Royal icing can be bought in specialty shops, but homemade royal icing is easy to mix and keeps well for several days in the refrigerator. Place in an airtight container and seal with plastic wrap so it doesn't dry out. Royal icing is good for spreading and piping and gradually sets hard. To stop this hardening, beat in 1 teaspoon of glycerin for each egg white used.

1. Put the egg white in a bowl with a little confectioners' sugar. Beat well until smooth.

2. Gradually beat in the remaining sugar to produce a soft, peaking consistency. Transfer to a container and cover tightly with plastic wrap. To color royal icing, use a toothpick to dot a little food coloring onto the icing and whisk in.

MAKES 1 QUANTITY

✦ Preparation time: 10 minutes

INGREDIENTS
* 1 egg white
* 1⅔ cups confectioners' sugar, sifted

Fondant

Ready-to-use fondant is available from specialty cake shops or the Internet. Homemade fondant can be stored for up to a week in a cool place, but it must be thoroughly wrapped in plastic wrap to prevent a crust from forming. Lightly knead before use.

1. Put the egg white, glucose, and 1 cup of the confectioners' sugar in a large bowl and mix with an electric mixer or wooden spoon until smooth.

2. Gradually work in more confectioners' sugar until the paste becomes too stiff to mix. Turn out onto a surface dusted with confectioners' sugar and gradually knead in more sugar with your hands until you have a smooth, firm paste. If it's too soft, the fondant will be sticky and difficult to roll out. Wrap thoroughly in plastic wrap until ready to use.

To color homemade fondant or store-bought ready-to-use fondant, dust a surface with confectioners' sugar and knead the paste lightly to soften. Dot the fondant with food coloring, using a toothpick. Knead until evenly colored, working in more color for a darker shade.

MAKES 1 lb 9 oz/700 g

✦ Preparation time: 15 minutes

INGREDIENTS
* 1 egg white
* 2 tbsp liquid glucose
* about 5 cups confectioners' sugar

USING CHOCOLATE

Chocolate is one of the most exciting cake ingredients to work with, not only for its delicious flavor and glossy texture but for its versatility as a frosting and decoration. Chocolate ganache, a chocolate cream frosting, makes a delicious covering for a cake, while melted chocolate can be shaped, molded, or piped into sculptural creations, both simple and intricate.

✳ Melting Chocolate

Chocolate can be melted in the microwave or on the stove top. Both methods work well, although you are better able to control the heating temperature of chocolate melted on the stove, particularly milk and white chocolate, which scorch easily if overheated.

To melt on the stove, chop the chocolate into small pieces and put in a heatproof bowl. Rest the bowl over a saucepan of gently simmering water, making sure that the bottom of the bowl does not sit in the water.

Once the chocolate starts to melt, turn off the heat and let stand until the chocolate is melted and smooth, stirring occasionally. Lift the bowl away from the pan, making sure that no drips of water get into the bowl because this will make the chocolate "seize," making it dull and solidified. To melt in the microwave, chop the chocolate, put in a microwave-proof bowl, and heat on medium power in 1-minute sessions, stirring gently after each heating so the chocolate melts evenly.

MAKES 1 QUANTITY

✦ Preparation time:
5 minutes, plus cooling

INGREDIENTS
✳ 9 oz/250 g semisweet dark chocolate, chopped
✳ 1 cup heavy cream
✳ 2 tbsp confectioners' sugar

Dark Chocolate Ganache

This luxurious frosting is a smooth blend of chocolate and cream. It is easiest to use once cooled and thickened but not starting to set. If it does firm up before you're ready to use it, place the bowl over a saucepan of hot water, stirring frequently until softened.

1. Put the chocolate in a bowl. Heat the cream and sugar in a saucepan until beginning to bubble around the edges (but not boiling), then pour over the chocolate.

2. Let stand, stirring frequently until the chocolate has melted and the ganache is smooth and glossy. It can be used as soon as it's cool enough to hold its shape.

For white chocolate ganache: Use the same quantites as dark, but heat only half of the cream to pour over the white chocolate. Once the chocolate has melted and the mixture is completely cold, stir in the remaining cream. Beat lightly with an electric mixer until the ganache just holds its shape. Do not overmix or the texture will be ruined.

✳ To Make Chocolate Curls

Use a vegetable peeler and pare off thick curls of chocolate from a bar. The curls can be made thicker by using a chunky bar of chocolate and by angling the peeler to get thicker curls.

If the chocolate is so cold that it breaks off in brittle pieces, warm very briefly for a few seconds in the microwave.

Chocolate caraque is another type of chocolate curl, usually reserved for special occasion cakes. See page 42 for how to make caraque.

✳ To Make a Chocolate Collar

A chocolate collar looks impressive encasing a special occasion cake. Before making the collar, have the cake ready on its serving plate or board and freshly spread with ganache, cream, or buttercream.

Measure around the circumference of the cake with a piece of string. Cut a piece of acetate that is ½ inch/1 cm longer than the string and ½ inch/1 cm deeper than the cake. Spread the acetate with melted semisweet dark, milk, or white chocolate, leaving ½ inch/1 cm uncovered at one short end. Spread the chocolate right to the edges of one long edge. The chocolate along the other edge can be spread in a wavy line or with a paintbrush to make an uneven edge. Let the collar rest on the acetate until the chocolate has thickened but is not beginning to set. It should take about 15 minutes, but keep lifting the edge of the collar to check how runny the chocolate is.

Lift the collar around the cake so the long, straight edge sits on the bottom. For larger cakes, you might need to ask someone to help you with positioning the collar. Secure the acetate at the ends with tape so the uncovered end overlaps the other. Let set completely in a cool place until the acetate can be peeled away.

CAKE-DECORATING TECHNIQUES

The following techniques are easy to master with practice. After covering with marzipan or fondant, the iced cakes should ideally be left overnight to set before decorating.

✳ Covering the Top with Marzipan

Apricot glaze is spread over cakes before adding marzipan, to hold the marzipan in place. To make, press the required amount of apricot preserves (see chosen recipe) through a strainer into a small saucepan and add 1 teaspoon of water or brandy for every 2 tablespoons of preserve. Heat gently until smooth.

Brush the top of the cake with the apricot glaze. Lightly knead the marzipan on a surface dusted with confectioners' sugar to soften. Reserve half of the marzipan, wrapped in plastic wrap, and roll out the remainder until 2 inches/5 cm larger than the diameter of the cake. Transfer to a sheet of parchment paper. Invert the cake onto the marzipan and press the paste up against the sides of the cake to fill the gaps around the edges. Use a sharp knife to cut off the excess marzipan to make a neat edge, reserving the trimmings. Turn the cake the right way up and place on a plate or cake board (see chosen recipe).

✳ Covering the Sides with Marzipan

Measure around the cake's circumference with a piece of string. Brush the sides of the cake with apricot glaze. Knead the trimmings with the reserved marzipan and roll out to a strip slightly longer than the string and slightly wider than the depth of the cake. Cut to the exact length and depth of the cake and roll up the paste. Place against the side of the cake and unroll, pressing it into position and butting the ends together.

✳ Covering with Fondant

Roll out the fondant on a surface lightly dusted with confectioners' sugar until 5 inches/13 cm larger than the diameter of the cake. Keep lifting and turning as you work so it doesn't stick. Using a rolling pin, lift the fondant over the cake so it falls evenly down the sides. Use your hands to ease the fondant around the cake so there are no creases and the fondant fits snugly around the bottom of the cake. Trim off excess with a knife held vertically against the side of the cake. Dust a fondant smoother with confectioners' sugar and use a circular motion to smooth the fondant flat on top, then around the sides. Keep working until the fondant is flat, trimming off any excess that builds up at the bottom. If any air bubbles appear, pop with a pin and resmooth. Let set overnight.

✳ Covering a Cake Board

Covering the exposed top edge of the cake board with fondant creates a professional-looking finish. Thinly roll out the required amount of fondant on a surface lightly dusted with confectioners' sugar to a long, thin, curved strip. Trim off the inner edge of the strip with a knife. Dampen the edges of the board with water and lift the strip into position so the cut edge rests against the side of the cake. Overlap the two ends and cut through with a knife. Lift away the trimmings and smooth out the seam with your fingers. Smooth the fondant around the edge of the board and trim off the excess with a knife.

✳ Basic Piping Techniques

Buttercream and ganache are easy to pipe, whether from a large or small piping tip. The consistency of royal icing can be altered according to the type of shapes to be piped. When piping stars, make sure that royal icing holds its shape when stirred with a spoon. Piping fine lines or tiny dots is easier to do if the icing is thinned with a few drops of water to form a softer consistency.

✳ Stacking Cakes

If you are making a three-tier stacked cake, it is best to use plastic dowels to provide support and prevent a potential collapse! Place a small bowl, plate, or cake board centered on the large cake and mark around it with the tip of a knife or artist's knife. Push a dowel down into the cake, just inside the marked circle, making sure it goes right through to the bottom of the cake. Make a pencil mark to show the height of the cake. Lift out the dowel and saw through the mark with a hacksaw or bread knife. Cut three more dowels to exactly the same height and push them into the cake, evenly spacing them inside the marked circle. Repeat the process with the middle tier. Spread some royal icing into the marked circles before stacking the cakes.

CUPCAKES & SMALL CAKES

1

Flower Cupcakes

MAKES 12

◆ Preparation time:
10 minutes, plus cooling
◆ Cooking time:
20–25 minutes
◆ Decoration time:
45 minutes

INGREDIENTS

✳ 1 quantity buttercream, see page 14
✳ black food coloring
✳ yellow food coloring
✳ 12 vanilla cupcakes, see page 12, baked in pink liners
✳ 1¾ oz/50 g black ready-to-use fondant, see page 15
✳ confectioners' sugar, for dusting
✳ 1¾ oz/50 g pink ready-to-use fondant, see page 15

The combination of pink, black, and yellow on these cupcakes is both modern and pretty, but you can choose any other colors to suit a particular occasion.

1. Place 2 tablespoons of the buttercream in a small bowl and beat in a little black food coloring. Put the remainder of the buttercream in a second bowl and beat in a little yellow food coloring. Set aside 2 tablespoons of the yellow buttercream. Using a palette knife, spread the bowl of yellow buttercream over the cupcakes, mounding it up slightly in domes in the centers.

2. Line a baking sheet with parchment paper. Thinly roll out the black fondant on a surface very lightly dusted with confectioners' sugar. Press a ½-inch/1-cm flower plunger cutter into the fondant. Lift away the cutter and transfer the fondant shapes to the prepared baking sheet, pressing out the shape with the plunger. Shape about 55 more black flowers in the same way.

3. Thinly roll out the pink fondant on a surface lightly dusted with confectioners' sugar. Create about 55 pink flowers, using the method in Step 2. Arrange all of the flowers over the buttercream, placing about nine on each cupcake.

4. Put the black buttercream and reserved yellow buttercream in two paper pastry bags (see page 9). Snip off just the very ends of the tips so that the fondant can be piped in tiny dots. Pipe a dot of black into the pink flowers and yellow into the black flowers.

HELPFUL HINT
The flowers can be shaped well in advance. Once hardened, store them in an airtight container between layers of paper towels for up to two weeks.

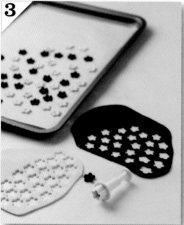

Animal Print Cupcakes

MAKES 12

♦ Preparation time:
10 minutes, plus cooling
♦ Cooking time:
20–25 minutes
♦ Decoration time:
1 hour

INGREDIENTS

✸ 12 chocolate cupcakes, see page 12, baked in black or brown liners
✸ 1 quantity chocolate buttercream, see page 14
✸ 3 oz/85 g black ready-to-use fondant, see page 15
✸ confectioners' sugar, for dusting
✸ 3 oz/85 g white ready-to use fondant, see page 15
✸ 3 oz/85 g brown ready-to-use fondant, see page 15
✸ 3 oz/85 g yellow ready-to-use fondant, see page 15

Bring a little animal magic to an afternoon snack with these fun cupcakes. Cute animal prints are rolled into contrasting colors of fondant to make professional-looking patterns.

1. Using a palette knife, spread the cupcakes with the buttercream in a fairly smooth layer.

2. Set aside a small, piece of the black fondant, then roll out the remainder thinly on a surface lightly dusted with confectioners' sugar. Place the fondant on a cutting board. Using a small, sharp knife, cut out small, wavy-edge shapes in varying sizes, ranging from about ½–1 inch/ 1–2.5 cm across. Make about 15 shapes and set aside any remaining trimmings. Set aside a small piece of white fondant and thinly roll out the remainder as above. Lay the black shapes over the white fondant, leaving a little space between each. Dust the rolling pin and roll it over the fondant so the black fondant is pressed into the white. Cut out circles with a 3-inch/ 7.5-cm round cutter from this black-and-white fondant and lay them over four of the cupcakes.

3. Set aside a small piece of brown fondant and thinly roll out the remainder, as above. Take the reserved black fondant, a small piece of yellow fondant, and the reserved white fondant and roll each with your fingers into long, thin ropes

(these can be of uneven thickness). Lay the ropes over the brown fondant in irregular lines. Roll, cut out circles using a 3-inch/7.5-cm round cutter, and lay them over another four cupcakes.

4. Thinly roll out the remaining yellow fondant, as before. Roll half of the reserved brown fondant into balls the size of small peas. Space them about 1½ inches/4 cm apart over the yellow fondant. Roll smaller balls of the remaining brown fondant (as small as you can) and position four of these tiny balls, about ¼ inch/5 mm apart, around one side of each of the pea-size balls. Roll, cut out circles, and position over the four remaining cupcakes, as before.

HELPFUL HINT
Use a very light dusting of confectioners' sugar when rolling black fondant, so it doesn't "cloud" the fondant.

Easter Chick Cupcakes

MAKES 12

◆ Preparation time:
10 minutes, plus cooling
◆ Cooking time:
20–25 minutes
◆ Decoration time:
1 hour, plus overnight
setting

INGREDIENTS

✳ 9 oz/250 g yellow
ready-to-use fondant,
see page 15
✳ confectioners' sugar,
for dusting
✳ 1 oz/30 g orange
ready-to-use fondant,
see page 15
✳ 7 oz/200 g white
chocolate
✳ blue food coloring
✳ 12 chocolate cupcakes,
see page 12, baked in
brown liners
✳ 1 quantity chocolate
buttercream, see page 14

These chirpy chicks provide a splash of color and fun—and are great as either a springtime or an Easter gift.

1. Trace and cut out the Easter chick template (see pages 94–95). Line a baking sheet with parchment paper. Thinly roll out half of the yellow fondant on a surface lightly dusted with confectioners' sugar and transfer to a cutting board. Lay the template over the fondant and carefully cut around it with an artist's knife or sharp knife. Cut five more chicks in the same way, transferring the shapes to the prepared baking sheet. Reroll the trimmings and the remaining yellow fondant and create another 7–8 chicks in the same way as above (the extras are in case of any breakages).

2. Roll out the orange fondant thinly on a surface lightly dusted with confectioners' sugar and cut out 14 small diamond shapes, using a sharp knife or artist's knife. Bend these diamonds almost in half and position on the chicks' heads, securing with a damp paintbrush. Let the chicks stand overnight to harden.

3. Use the white chocolate to make white chocolate curls (see page 17).

4. Dilute a little blue food coloring with a drop of water and use to paint eyes on the chicks. Using a palette knife, spread the cupcakes with the buttercream. While the buttercream is still soft, peel the paper away from the chicks and press the chicks gently down onto the cupcakes so they are held in place by the buttercream. Scatter the chocolate curls around the chicks.

HELPFUL HINT
If you are not confident with painting the eyes with a brush, try using a blue icing pen, available from specialty cake shops.

New Baby Cupcakes

MAKES 12

✦ Preparation time:
10 minutes, plus cooling

✦ Cooking time:
20–25 minutes

✦ Decoration time:
1 hour

INGREDIENTS

✳ 5½ oz/150 g white
ready-to-use fondant,
see page 15

✳ confectioners' sugar,
for dusting

✳ 5½ oz/150 g pale blue
or pink ready-to-use
fondant, see page 15

✳ 1 tbsp apricot
preserves

✳ 12 vanilla cupcakes,
see page 12, baked in blue
or pink liners

✳ tube of white
writing icing

These pretty cupcakes can be made with either pink or blue fondant to suit the gender of the new baby—or any other color that you prefer!

1. Thinly roll out the white fondant on a surface lightly dusted with confectioners' sugar. Using a 3-inch/7.5-cm cutter, stamp out six rounds. Repeat with the blue or pink fondant. Make apricot glaze with the preserves (see page 18). Brush each cupcake lightly with a little of the glaze and gently press a fondant round on top.

2. Reroll the blue or pink fondant trimmings. Use a small teddy bear cutter to stamp out two teddy bears. Use a tiny flower cutter to stamp out four flowers.

3. Reroll the white fondant trimmings. Use a small flower cutter to stamp out two small flowers. Use a 1½-inch/4-cm fluted cutter to stamp out two rounds, then cut away a small oval from each round to resemble a baby's bib. Use a 1-inch/2.5-cm cutter to stamp out two rounds and mark with the end of a paintbrush to resemble buttons. Shape four booties and two ducks from the remaining fondant trimmings.

4. Attach all the decorations to the top of the cupcakes using a damp paintbrush. Use the writing icing to add the finishing touches, such as bows on the booties.

HELPFUL HINT
The decorations can be adapted to suit whichever cutters you already have in your kitchen drawer.

Cupcake Wedding Cake

MAKES 36

◆ Preparation time:
30 minutes, plus cooling
◆ Cooking time:
1–1¼ hours
◆ Decoration time:
1½ hours

INGREDIENTS

✹ 36 vanilla cupcakes,
see page 12, baked in
white liners
✹ 2 quantities
buttercream, see page 14
✹ 1 lb 12 oz/800 g white
ready-to-use fondant,
see page 15
✹ confectioners' sugar,
for dusting
✹ 3½ oz/100 g green
ready-to-use fondant,
see page 15

Anyone can tackle decorating a wedding cake when it's made entirely of cupcakes! Multiply the quantity of cakes so it's right for the number of guests and change the bow colors to tie in with the colors being used for the wedding decorations.

1. Using a palette knife, cover the cupcakes with buttercream in a fairly smooth layer. Thinly roll out one third of the white fondant on a surface lightly dusted with confectioners' sugar. Cut out circles using a 3-inch/7.5-cm round cutter and press gently onto the cupcakes. Gather up the trimmings and reroll with another one third of the fondant until all of the cupcakes are covered.

2. To make the bows, roll out about one quarter of the remaining white fondant, as above, to a 6-inch/15-cm square. Thinly roll out one quarter of the green fondant until 6 inches/ 15 cm long. Cut into ¼-inch/5-mm strips and lay the strips over the white fondant, leaving a tiny gap between each.

3. Roll the rolling pin over the fondant to flatten the green fondant into the white.

4. Use a sharp knife to cut vertically down the middle of the green parts of the fondant to create green-edge lengths of fondant. For each bow, cut two 1-inch/2.5-cm lengths from the fondant and place on a cupcake for bow ends, securing in place with a damp paintbrush. Cut two 2-inch/5-cm lengths, bend into loops, pinching the ends together, and position above the bow ends. Secure as above. Cut another ½-inch/1-cm square of fondant, shape into a cube, and position in the middle of the bow to form the knot. Secure as above. Repeat with the remaining cut fondant lengths, then roll and shape more bows using the remaining fondant until all the cupcakes are decorated.

HELPFUL HINT
These cakes look stunning arranged on a tiered cupcake or cake stand. Arrange a posy of small white flowers in the center of the tiers.

Snowflake Cupcakes

MAKES 12

✦ Preparation time:
10 minutes, plus cooling
✦ Cooking time:
20–25 minutes
✦ Decoration time:
1½ hours, plus 24 hours
setting

INGREDIENTS
❋ 2 quantities royal icing,
see page 15
❋ edible white
glitter flakes
❋ finely grated rind and
juice of 2 limes
❋ 3 tbsp superfine sugar
❋ 12 vanilla cupcakes,
see page 12, baked in
blue liners
❋ 3 tbsp lime or lemon
preserves
❋ 8 oz/225 g marzipan
❋ confectioners' sugar,
for dusting

These delicate snowflake cakes, dusted with sparkling glitter, will take pride of place on the kitchen table. Don't be put off by the intricate style of the piping—once you've done one, the rest will definitely get easier!

1. Line a large baking sheet or board with parchment paper. Trace the snowflake template (see pages 94–95) and slide the traced template under the parchment paper. Take one quarter of the royal icing and check that it is the right consistency for piping (see page 19). Spoon this icing into a pastry bag fitted with a writer tip (see page 9). Pipe over all the lines of the snowflake template and scatter with edible glitter flakes while still soft. Move the template around and pipe 12–13 more snowflake shapes onto the parchment paper. Let stand to harden for 24 hours.

2. Heat the lime rind and juice in a small saucepan with the superfine sugar until dissolved. Using a skewer, pierce holes all over the cupcakes and drizzle with the syrup. Press the preserves through a strainer into the pan and add 1 tablespoon of water. Heat gently until the preserves have melted. Brush the mixture over the cupcakes.

3. Thinly roll out the marzipan on a surface lightly dusted with confectioners' sugar. Cut out circles using a 7.5-cm/3-inch round cutter and lay them over the cupcakes, rerolling the trimmings to make more rounds.

4. Using a palette knife, spread the remaining royal icing over the cupcakes. Carefully peel the parchment paper away from the snowflakes and place the snowflakes gently on each cupcake.

HELPFUL HINT
You'll need 12 snowflakes in total but it's worth piping two or three extra in case of breakages. Always peel the paper away from delicate decorating shapes—instead of the shape away from the paper—to avoid breaking them.

Lemon & Almond Fondants

MAKES 16

✦ Preparation time:
15 minutes, plus cooling
✦ Cooking time:
25–30 minutes
✦ Decoration time:
1½ hours, plus setting

INGREDIENTS

✹ ¾ cup lightly
salted butter, softened,
plus extra for greasing
✹ 1 cup superfine sugar
✹ 3 eggs
✹ 1¼ cup self-rising flour
✹ 1 tsp almond extract
✹ ⅓ cup ground almonds

TO DECORATE

✹ ¼ cup superfine sugar
✹ 3 tbsp lemon juice
✹ 1 quantity lemon
buttercream, see page 14
✹ 4 cups confectioners'
sugar
✹ yellow and pink
food coloring
✹ 8 pale yellow and
8 pale pink sugar roses,
see page 76

These little cakes are just perfect for a special gathering. They also make a great present, arranged in a shallow box.

1. Preheat the oven to 350°F/180°C. Grease and line two 7-inch/18-cm square layer cake pans (see page 7). Put the butter, superfine sugar, eggs, flour, almond extract, and ground almonds in a bowl and beat with a handheld electric mixer until smooth and creamy. Divide the batter between the prepared pans and bake in the preheated oven for 25–30 minutes, or until just firm to the touch. Transfer to a wire rack to cool.

2. To decorate, mix together the superfine sugar and lemon juice. Let stand for 10 minutes, or until the sugar dissolves. Sandwich the cakes together with half of the buttercream and spoon the lemon syrup over the top. Using a large, sharp knife, trim off a ¼-inch/5-mm slice from the edges of the cake, then cut the cake into 16 squares.

3. Using a palette knife, spread the remaining buttercream on top of each square, mounding the buttercream up in the center into a dome.

4. Beat the confectioners' sugar with about 5–6 tablespoons of cold water to make a smooth paste that thickly coats the back of a metal spoon. Divide between two bowls and color half of the paste pale yellow and half pale pink.

5. Place the squares on a wire rack. Using a teaspoon, drizzle the yellow icing over eight cakes so it runs down the sides, coating most of the cake (don't worry if there are areas of cake still visible). Cover the remaining cakes with pink icing. Let the squares set, then decorate with the sugar roses.

HELPFUL HINT
If made a day in advance, the cake will be much easier to cut and decorate.

Chocolate Ice-Cream Cones

MAKES 8

◆ Preparation time:
45 minutes
◆ Cooking time:
20–25 minutes
◆ Decoration time:
30 minutes

INGREDIENTS
✳ 1 egg white
✳ ¼ cup packed light brown sugar
✳ 1 tbsp all-purpose flour
✳ 2 tbsp unsweetened cocoa
✳ 2 tbsp heavy cream
✳ 2 tbsp butter, melted
✳ 1 quantity dark chocolate ganache, see page 16
✳ 3½ oz/100 g store-bought chocolate cake
✳ sugar sprinkles, to decorate

Crisp chocolate wafer cones, filled with chocolate cake and creamy chocolate ganache, will make an indulgent fix for any serious chocolate lover!

1. Preheat the oven to 400°F/200°C. To make the cones, line a baking sheet with parchment paper. Put the egg white and sugar in a bowl and whisk until combined. Add the flour, cocoa, cream, and butter and mix to a smooth paste.

2. Place 2 tablespoons of the batter, spaced well apart, on the prepared sheet. Spread each portion of batter with the back of a spoon into a round about 4½ inches/12 cm in diameter.

3. Bake in the preheated oven for 5–6 minutes until the surface looks dry and has slight bubbles in it. Let cool for 1 minute. Peel away each round from the paper and roll into a cone shape. As each cone cools, it will start to firm up; you might find it easier to push a cone of paper towel into the chocolate cone and let it support the shape until it cools. Repeat with a second batch, then bake and shape in the same way, using new parchment paper each time. Repeat to create eight cones in total.

4. Put the ganache into a large pastry bag fitted with a ½-inch/1-cm star tip (see page 9). Pipe a little into each cone until about one-third full. Spread this up the sides with a knife so the insides of the cones are covered in a thin layer of ganache. Crumble the chocolate cake into the prepared chocolate cones.

5. Pipe large swirls of the remaining chocolate ganache into the tops of the cones and finish with sugar sprinkles.

HELPFUL HINT
If the cones cool before you have a chance to shape them, put them back very briefly in the oven to soften, so they are easier to roll up.

CAKES FOR ALL OCCASIONS

2

Frosted Fruits Cake

SERVES 16

✦ Preparation time:
25 minutes, plus cooling

✦ Cooking time:
35–40 minutes

✦ Decoration time:
40 minutes, plus chilling

INGREDIENTS

✹ 2 vanilla layer cakes,
8 inches/20 cm in
diameter, see page 11

✹ 5 tbsp raspberry or
strawberry preserves

✹ ⅔ cup heavy cream

✹ pink food coloring

✹ 2 quantities cream
cheese frosting,
see page 14

✹ 3–3½ cups mixed
berries, such as
strawberries, raspberries,
and blueberries

✹ confectioners' sugar,
for sprinkling

This impressive cake is perfect for a summer afternoon treat or as a dessert after a leisurely lunch. Use firm, undamaged fruits so their juices don't seep into the frosting.

1. Place one of the cakes on a flat serving plate and spread with the preserves. Using an electric mixer, whip the cream until it is just holding its shape. Spread the cream over the preserves, almost to the edges of the cake. Position the second cake on top and press down gently so the cream is level with the edges of the cake.

2. Beat a dash of pink food coloring into the cream cheese frosting to color it the palest shade of pink. Using a palette knife, spread a very thin layer over the top and sides of the cake to seal in the crumbs. The cake will still show through at this stage, but it will be covered by the second layer of frosting. Chill in the refrigerator for 15 minutes.

3. Use the palette knife to spread a thicker layer of frosting around the sides of the cake. Spread the remainder over the top. Once evenly covered, use the edge of the palette knife to smooth the frosting as flat or as textured as you like.

4. Arrange the fruit on top of the cake. Put a little confectioners' sugar in a small, fine strainer or dredger and gently tap it over the fruit to lightly frost.

HELPFUL HINT
Once frosted, this cake can be stored in a cool place, preferably not the refrigerator, for 24 hours before decorating and serving.

Chocolate Caraque Cake

◆ Preparation time:
25 minutes, plus cooling

◆ Cooking time:
2 hours

◆ Decoration time:
35 minutes, plus chilling

INGREDIENTS

✳ 7 oz/200 g semisweet dark chocolate, chopped

✳ 1 rich chocolate cake, 8 inches/20 cm in diameter, see page 10

✳ 6 tbsp brandy (optional)

✳ 2 quantities dark chocolate ganache, see page 16

✳ rose petals or small edible flowers, to decorate (optional)

Making chocolate caraque is a baking skill that's easy to achieve and adds a professional-looking touch to cakes and desserts. Caraque can be stored in an airtight container for two weeks without spoiling, layered between sheets of parchment paper.

1. Melt the chocolate (see page 16) and spread it in a thin layer on a marble slab or clean, smooth surface, such as a plastic cutting board. Let stand in a cool place until the chocolate is set but not brittle.

2. Push a clean wallpaper scraper or the edge of a palette knife across the surface of the chocolate, holding it at an angle of about 30 degrees so that the chocolate starts to roll into loose curls. If the chocolate is too cold, it will break off in brittle shards; let it stand at room temperature for a while before trying again. Transfer the caraque to a baking sheet lined with parchment paper and chill in the refrigerator while you finish the cake.

3. Slice the cake in half horizontally. Drizzle the tops of the cake halves with brandy, if using.

4. Use one quarter of the chocolate ganache to sandwich the cake layers together and place the cake on a flat serving plate or cake stand. Spread a thin layer of ganache around the sides of the cake with a palette knife to seal in the crumbs. Chill in the refrigerator for 15 minutes. Spread the remaining ganache all over the cake in an even layer, smoothing it until it is as flat or as textured as you like.

5. Scatter the chocolate caraque over the cake so the pieces fall at different angles. Scatter with rose petals or small edible flowers, if using.

HELPFUL HINT
A small marble slab is a worthwhile investment if you do a lot of chocolate work, because its cool surface helps chocolate to set.

Chocolate Ganache Cake

SERVES 10

✦ Preparation time:
25 minutes, plus cooling
✦ Cooking time:
40 minutes
✦ Decoration time:
1 hour, plus chilling

INGREDIENTS

✹ ¾ cup butter,
plus extra for greasing
✹ ¾ cup superfine sugar
✹ 4 eggs, lightly beaten
✹ 2 cups self-rising flour
✹ 1 tbsp unsweetened
cocoa
✹ 9 oz/250 g semisweet
dark chocolate
✹ 2 quantities dark
chocolate ganache, see
page 16

This simple and light chocolate cake looks visually impressive with the piped ganache topping and a chocolate collar arranged around the outside.

1. Preheat the oven to 350°F/180°C. Grease and line the bottom of an 8-inch/20-cm round springform cake pan (see page 7).

2. Beat the butter and sugar until light and fluffy. Gradually add the eggs, beating well after each addition. Sift the flour and cocoa together. Fold into the cake mixture. Melt 2 squares of the dark chocolate (see page 16), then fold the melted chocolate into the cake batter. Spoon into the prepared pan and smooth the top. Bake in the preheated oven for 40 minutes, or until springy to the touch. Let the cake cool for 5 minutes, then turn out onto a wire rack. Cut into two layers.

3. Reserve one third of the dark chocolate ganache. Use the remaining ganache to sandwich the cake together and spread over the top and sides of the cake.

4. Chop the remaining chocolate, melt it (see page 16), and use to create a chocolate collar around the cake (see page 17). Let cool until just set. Make a paper pastry bag (see page 9) and pipe the reserved ganache onto the cake in teardrop shapes.

HELPFUL HINT
Wait for 2 hours, or until the ganache is firm, light, and fluffy, before piping the shapes over the cake.

Coffee Bundt Cake

SERVES 12–14

✦ Preparation time:
30 minutes, plus cooling
✦ Cooking time:
50 minutes
✦ Decoration time:
20 minutes

INGREDIENTS

✳ 3¼ cups all-purpose flour, plus extra for dusting
✳ 1 tbsp baking powder
✳ 1 tsp baking soda
✳ 3 tbsp instant espresso coffee powder
✳ 1¼ cups butter, softened, plus extra for greasing
✳ ½ cup packed light brown sugar
✳ 1 cup maple syrup
✳ 3 eggs, beaten
✳ 1 cup buttermilk
✳ 1 cup heavy cream

TO DECORATE

✳ 4 tbsp maple syrup
✳ 1⅔ cups confectioners' sugar
✳ 1 tbsp unsalted butter, melted
✳ 20 chocolate-coated coffee beans

Bundt cakes cook quickly and, therefore, stay deliciously moist because of the hole through the center of the pan. The flavor combination of coffee and maple syrup is just delicious!

1. Preheat the oven to 350°F/180°C. Grease a 3-quart/3-liter Bundt pan. Dust the bottom and sides with flour, tipping out the excess.

2. Sift the flour, baking powder, baking soda, and coffee powder into a bowl. In a separate bowl, beat together the butter and brown sugar with an electric mixer until pale and creamy. Gradually beat in the maple syrup. Beat in the eggs slowly, adding 3 tablespoons of the flour mixture to prevent curdling.

3. Mix together the buttermilk and cream and add half to the butter mixture. Sprinkle in half of the flour mixture and fold gently together. Add the remaining buttermilk and flour mixtures and mix together gently until just combined.

4. Spoon into the prepared pan and smooth the surface. Bake in the preheated oven for about 50 minutes, or until well risen and a skewer inserted into the center comes out clean. Let stand in the pan for 10 minutes, then loosen with a knife and invert onto a wire rack to cool completely.

5. To make the icing, beat the maple syrup in a bowl with 1¼ cups of the confectioners' sugar and the butter, until smooth and thickly coating the back of a wooden spoon. Transfer the cake to a serving plate and spoon the icing around the top of the cake so it starts to run down the sides.

6. Beat the remaining confectioners' sugar in a small bowl with 1½–2 teaspoons of water to make a smooth paste. Using a teaspoon, drizzle the icing over the cake. Scatter the coffee beans over the top.

HELPFUL HINT
If you don't have a classic Bundt pan, use any other tube pan with the same capacity.

3

5

6

Flower Power

SERVES 12–14

◆ Preparation time:
25 minutes, plus cooling

◆ Cooking time:
40 minutes

◆ Decoration time:
1 hour, plus overnight
setting

INGREDIENTS

✺ 2 carrot cakes, see
page 12

✺ 1 quantity buttercream,
see page 14

✺ 1 lb 9 oz/700 g lime
green ready-to-use
fondant, see page 15

✺ 5½ oz/150 g white
ready-to-use fondant,
if covering cake board,
see page 15

✺ 2½ oz/70 g each of
white, pink, orange, and
yellow ready-to-use
fondant, see page 15

✺ confectioners' sugar,
for dusting

✺ small bowl of pink,
yellow, and orange candy-
coated chocolate candies

✺ 1 yard/1 m pink
or yellow ribbon,
½ inch/1 cm wide
(optional)

This funky, fun cake will appeal to every girl from 1 to 91! Once decorated, it will keep in a cool place for several days.

1. Sandwich the two carrot cakes together with half of the buttercream. Place on a 11-inch/28-cm round cake board (or use a flat plate that complements the colors of the decoration). Spoon 3 tablespoons of the buttercream into a small paper pastry bag fitted with a writer tip (see page 9). Using a palette knife, spread the remaining buttercream over the top and sides of the cake.

2. Use the lime green fondant to cover the cake (see page 18) and the white fondant to cover the cake board, if using (see page 19). Let stand overnight, until firm, before decorating, if desired.

3. Thinly roll out the white, pink, orange, and yellow fondant on a surface lightly dusted with confectioners' sugar. Cut out flower shapes with a selection of cutters (see Helpful Hint).

4. Secure the flowers to the cake by moistening the backs of the flowers with a damp paintbrush and pressing gently onto the fondant. Build up the design into a trail that curls into a point on the top of the cake and thickens out around the sides. The design will start to look effective as you add more flowers to the cake, mixing up the colors and shapes.

5. Secure the candies in the center of some of the flowers with dots of buttercream from the pastry bag. Add dots of buttercream to the centers of the remaining flowers. Wrap the ribbon around the cake board, if using, securing with a straight pin.

HELPFUL HINT
Use flower cutters in 4–5 different sizes and, for the best effect, use a mixture of fluted and pointed cutters.

3

4

5

Shopper's Heaven

SERVES 16

◆ Preparation time:
25 minutes, plus cooling
◆ Cooking time:
35–40 minutes
◆ Decoration time:
1¼ hours, plus overnight setting

INGREDIENTS

✹ 2 lemon layer cakes,
7 inches/18 cm square,
see page 11
✹ 1 quantity lemon
buttercream, see page 14
✹ 6 tbsp lemon curd
✹ 1 lb 12 oz/800 g white
ready-to-use fondant,
see page 15
✹ 5½ oz/150 g black
ready-to-use fondant,
see page 15
✹ 3 oz/85 g each of deep
pink, pale gray, and green
ready-to-use fondant,
see page 15
✹ confectioners' sugar,
for dusting
✹ ½ quantity royal icing,
see page 15
✹ black food coloring
✹ 1 yard/1 m pink or gray
ribbon, ½ inch/1 cm wide

Do you have a friend who thrives on retail therapy? This could be the perfect cake choice to entice her away from the stores! Dresses, shoes, and purses look effective, but you can easily create your own designs.

1. Sandwich the cakes together with half of the buttercream and all of the lemon curd. Place the cake on an 11-inch/28-cm square cake board. Using a palette knife, spread the remaining buttercream over the top and sides of the cake.

2. Use the white fondant to cover the cake (see page 18) and the black fondant to cover the cake board (see page 19). Let stand overnight, until firm, before decorating, if desired.

3. Trace and cut out the dress, shoe, and purse templates (see pages 94–95). Thinly roll out half of the pink, gray, and green fondants on a surface lightly dusted with confectioners' sugar and transfer to a cutting board. Lay the templates over the fondant and cut around each with an artist's knife or sharp knife. Repeat with the remaining fondants.

4. Once you've cut several shapes, moisten the backs with a damp paintbrush and press them gently onto the cake, leaving a small gap between them. Cover the rest of the cake in the same way, trimming off the shapes with an artist's knife where they extend past the bottom of the cake.

5. Color the royal icing black (see page 15) and put into a pastry bag fitted with a writer tip (see page 9). Pipe buttons onto the dresses and details on the purses. Wrap the ribbon around the cake board, securing with a straight pin.

HELPFUL HINT
A lightweight, plastic cutting board is ideal for cutting out fondant shapes with an artist's knife. If it slips on the counter, rest it on a dish towel.

Chocolate Drizzle Cake

SERVES 20

◆ Preparation time:
40 minutes, plus cooling

◆ Cooking time:
1½ hours

◆ Decoration time:
45 minutes, plus setting

INGREDIENTS

✳ 2 rich chocolate cakes, 6 inches/15 cm in diameter, see page 10

✳ 2 quantities white chocolate ganache, see page 16

✳ 1 tbsp unsalted butter

✳ 1 tbsp light corn syrup

✳ 3½ oz/100 g semisweet dark chocolate, chopped

✳ 14 oz–1 lb 2 oz/ 400 g–500 g semisweet dark, milk, and white chocolate truffles

Our love affair with chocolate is exemplified in this party centerpiece—an intensely decadent creation, from the richly flavored cake to its lavish decoration.

1. Slice each cake in half horizontally and sandwich all the layers together with one quarter of the chocolate ganache. Place all the layers on a flat serving plate.

2. Spread a thin layer of ganache around the sides of the cake with a palette knife to seal in the crumbs. Chill in the refrigerator for 15 minutes. Spread the remaining ganache all over the sides in an even layer. Let stand in a cool place for at least an hour, until firm.

3. Put the butter and syrup in a small saucepan and heat gently until the butter has melted. Add the chocolate and heat very gently until the chocolate starts to melt. Remove from the heat and stir until the chocolate has melted completely. Spoon into a small bowl and let stand until cool and slightly thickened but not starting to set.

4. Pour the chocolate over the top of the cake and ease it to the edges with a palette knife. Use the back of a teaspoon to gently nudge the chocolate over the edges of the cake so it starts to run down the sides. Repeat all around the top of the cake.

5. Let stand in a cool place for at least an hour, until firm, before piling the chocolate truffles on top.

HELPFUL HINT

This cake looks most effective if the chocolate is drizzled down the sides unevenly. Do this by nudging various amounts of the chocolate mixture over the top edges of the cake.

Chocolate Tiered Cake

SERVES 34

◆ Preparation time:
1 hour, plus cooling
◆ Cooking time:
3¾ hours
◆ Decoration time:
1¼ hours, plus overnight
setting

INGREDIENTS
✱ 2 quantities dark
chocolate ganache,
see page 16
✱ 8 chocolate cupcakes,
see page 12, baked in
blue liners
✱ 2 rich chocolate cakes,
10 inches/25 cm and
4 inches/10 cm in
diameter, see page 10
✱ 3 lb/1.3 kg store-
bought, ready-to-use
chocolate fondant
✱ confectioners' sugar,
for dusting
✱ 3½ oz/100 g each of
blue and green ready-to-
use fondant, see page 15
✱ handful of blue, green,
and brown sugar-coated
chocolate candies
✱ 20 inches/50 cm blue
ribbon, ½ inch/1 cm wide

This colorful, fun cake offers guests the choice between either a ganache-laden cupcake or a chunky slice of chocolate cake.

1. Put one third of the chocolate ganache in a large pastry bag fitted with a ½-inch/1-cm star tip (see page 9) and pipe swirls onto the cupcakes. Place the large chocolate cake on a 13-inch/33-cm cake board. Put the small chocolate cake on a baking sheet lined with parchment paper.

2. Spread the remaining ganache over the top and sides of both cakes, using a palette knife to spread it in a smooth layer.

3. Thinly roll out two thirds of the chocolate fondant on a surface lightly dusted with confectioners' sugar and use to cover the large cake (see page 18). Reserve the trimmings. Cover the small cake with two thirds of the remaining chocolate fondant. After you trim off the excess fondant from around the bottom, carefully position the small cake on top of the large one, in the center. Use the trimmings and the remaining fondant to cover the cake board (see page 19). Let stand overnight, until firm, before decorating, if desired.

4. Thinly roll out half of the blue and green fondants, as before, and cut out a selection of circles, using small round cutters. Position them around the sides of the cakes, securing in place with a damp paintbrush. Roll out any trimmings and the remaining fondants to make more circles.

5. Arrange seven of the cupcakes around the edge of the lower tier and one on the top tier, scattering them with the candies. Wrap the blue ribbon around the bottom of the larger cake and the cake board, securing with straight pins.

HELPFUL HINT
The blue and green decorations look great against the chocolate fondant but you can adapt the colors to suit.

Pretty In Pink

SERVES 24

◆ Preparation time:
45 minutes, plus cooling

◆ Cooking time:
1 hour

◆ Decoration time:
2 hours, plus overnight setting

INGREDIENTS

✺ 4 vanilla layer cakes,
2 x 8 inches/20 cm and
2 x 6 inches/15 cm in diameter, see page 11

✺ ½ cup raspberry or strawberry preserves

✺ 2 quantities buttercream, see page 14

✺ 1 lb 9 oz/ 700 g pale pink ready-to-use fondant, see page 15

✺ confectioners' sugar, for dusting

✺ 1 lb 12 oz/800 g deep pink ready-to-use fondant, see page 15

✺ ½ quantity royal icing, see page 15

✺ 1½ yards /1.5 m pale cream ribbon, ½ inch/
1 cm wide

✺ bag of pearl balls

✺ 1 yard/1 m fluffy pink trim

This cute cake will impress any young girl for a variety of occasions. Simple hearts and pearl balls are easy to secure, making it well within the grasp of first-time decorators.

1. Sandwich the large cakes together with ⅓ cup of the preserves and ½ cup of the buttercream and place on a 10-inch/25-cm round cake board. Sandwich the small cakes together with the remaining preserves and another ⅓ cup of the buttercream. Place on a 6-inch/15-cm cake board.

2. Using a palette knife, spread the tops and sides of both cakes with the remaining buttercream. Use the pale pink fondant to cover the large cake (see page 18). Dust a surface lightly with confectioners' sugar and roll out two thirds of the deep pink fondant. Use this deep pink fondant to cover the small cake (see page 18). Put a teaspoon of the royal icing on the center of the large cake and spread it slightly. Position the small cake on top. Use about two thirds of the remaining deep pink fondant to cover the cake board (see page 19). Let stand overnight, until firm, before decorating, if desired.

3. Put the remaining royal icing in a paper pastry bag (see page 9) and snip off just the tip. Wrap the cream ribbon around the bottom of the small cake so it overlaps slightly. Trim and set aside the remaining ribbon. Secure the ribbon around the small cake with a dot of royal icing.

4. Thinly roll out half of the remaining deep pink fondant and cut out small heart shapes, using ½-inch/1-cm and ¾-inch/2-cm heart-shape cutters. Moisten the backs of the hearts with a damp paintbrush and secure over the large cake. Gather up the trimmings and roll out with the remaining deep pink fondant and cut out another 2–3 heart shapes, using a slightly larger cutter. Place on a sheet of parchment paper to harden for at least 2 hours.

5. Pipe small dots of royal icing, about ½ inch/1 cm apart, onto the small cake and press a pearl ball gently onto each. Wrap more cream ribbon around the cake board, securing with a straight pin.

6. Secure the pink trim around the large cake with a dot of royal icing. Coil more pink trim on top of the cake, securing with royal icing and tucking in the large pink hearts to finish.

Giant Cupcake

SERVES 10

◆ Preparation time:
20 minutes, plus cooling

◆ Cooking time:
1¼ hours

◆ Decoration time:
1¼ hours, plus overnight setting

INGREDIENTS
✺ butter, for greasing
✺ 1 quantity rich chocolate cake batter, 6 inches/15 cm in diameter, see page 10, uncooked
✺ 1 quantity chocolate buttercream, see page 14
✺ 1 lb 2 oz/500 g blue ready-to-use fondant, see page 15
✺ confectioners' sugar, for dusting
✺ ½ oz/15 g each of pink, blue, white, and yellow ready-to-use fondant, see page 15
✺ 1¼ cups confectioners' sugar
✺ 1 oz/30 g red ready-to-use fondant, see page 15
✺ confectioners' glaze, see Helpful Hint

This must be the only cupcake in the world to serve 10 hungry cake lovers!

1. Preheat the oven to 325°F/160°C Grease and line a 1-quart/1-liter deep, dome-shape ovenproof bowl with wax paper. Spoon the cake batter into the bowl and bake in the preheated oven for 1¼ hours, or until a skewer inserted into the center comes out clean. Let cool in the bowl.

2. Slice the domed surface off the top of the cake and crumble into a bowl. Beat 3 tablespoons of the buttercream into the bowl, cover, and set aside in a cool place. Invert the remaining cake onto a cutting board lined with parchment paper and spread with the remaining buttercream. Roll out the blue fondant on a surface dusted with confectioners' sugar to a 12-inch/30-cm round. Lift the fondant over the cake and ease it to fit neatly around the sides. Trim off the excess around the bottom. While the fondant is still soft, take an unridged pencil and press it into the fondant all around the sides to create grooves.

3. Roll the pink, blue, white, and yellow fondants as thinly as possible under your fingers. Cut into irregular lengths to shape giant sprinkles. Place on a sheet of parchment paper or board and let both the cake and sprinkles harden overnight.

4. Turn the cake the right way up and place on a plate. Pack the cake crumbs mixture onto the top of the cake, mounding it into a dome in the center similar to the original cake shape.

5. Beat the confectioners' sugar with about 5 teaspoons of cold water to make a slightly runny paste. Spoon over the top of the cake and scatter with the giant sprinkles. Roll the red fondant into a ball and position on top of the cake. Brush with confectioners' glaze.

HELPFUL HINT
Confectioners' glaze, available from cake-decorating websites, is used to create a glossy sheen, or you could brush with honey instead.

2

3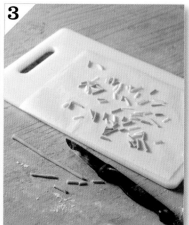

4

Grasshopper Cake

SERVES 8

◆ Preparation time:
25 minutes, plus cooling

◆ Cooking time:
1¼ hours

◆ Decoration time:
20 minutes

INGREDIENTS
✳ 1 cup milk
✳ 1 tbsp lemon juice
✳ 2¼ cups self-rising flour
✳ 2 tbsp unsweetened cocoa
✳ 1 tsp baking soda
✳ ½ cup butter, softened, plus extra for greasing
✳ 1 cup superfine sugar
✳ 2 extra large eggs
✳ 3½ oz/100 g semisweet dark chocolate, melted
✳ 1 oz/25 g milk chocolate, grated, to decorate

FROSTING
✳ 1 cup unsalted butter, softened
✳ 1 cup heavy cream
✳ 3¼ cups confectioners' sugar, sifted
✳ 1 tsp peppermint extract
✳ few drops of green food coloring

Named after a Crème de Menthe cocktail, this decadent gateau is made up of layers of rich, moist chocolate cake with a creamy mint-flavored buttercream.

1. Preheat the oven to 325°F/160°C. Grease and line an 8-inch/20-cm round deep cake cake pan (see page 7).

2. Pour the milk into a pitcher and add the lemon juice. Let stand for 15 minutes—the milk will start to curdle but this is okay.

3. Sift the flour, unsweetened cocoa, and baking soda into a large bowl. Add the butter, superfine sugar, and eggs and pour in the milk mixture. Beat with an electric handheld mixer until thoroughly combined. Whisk in the melted chocolate.

4. Spoon the batter into the prepared pan and smooth the surface. Bake in the preheated oven for about 1¼ hours, or until the cake is risen and a skewer inserted into the center comes out clean. Cool in the pan for 20 minutes, then turn out onto a wire rack to cool completely.

5. For the buttercream frosting, place the butter in a bowl and beat with an electric handheld mixer for 2–3 minutes, until pale and creamy. Beat in two thirds of the cream, then gradually beat in the confectioners' sugar. Add the rest of the cream and continue beating for 1–2 minutes, until the buttercream is very light and fluffy. Stir in the peppermint extract and enough food coloring to produce a pale green color.

6. Slice the cake horizontally into three equal rounds. Sandwich the rounds together with half of the buttercream. Spread the remaining buttercream over the top and sides of the cake. Decorate with the grated chocolate.

HELPFUL HINT
For an alcoholic version, flavor the buttercream with a couple of spoonfuls of Crème de Menthe instead of the peppermint extract.

CELEBRATION CAKES

3

Chocolate Birthday Cake

SERVES 34

◆ Preparation time:
1 hour, plus cooling
◆ Cooking time:
4½ hours
◆ Decoration time:
2 hours, plus overnight setting

INGREDIENTS

✹ 3½ oz/100 g each of semisweet dark, milk, and white chocolate, chopped and kept separate
✹ 3 rich chocolate cakes, 8 inches/20 cm, 6 inches/15 cm, and 4 inches/10 cm in diameter, see page 10
✹ 1 quantity white chocolate ganache, see page 16
✹ 3 quantities dark chocolate ganache, see page 16

With minor adjustments, this fabulous chocolate-packed, coming-of-age cake can be adapted to suit any birthday by simply using the appropriate numbers to replace the 2s and 1s.

1. Line a baking sheet or cutting board with parchment paper. Melt the dark chocolate (see page 16). Trace ten each of the "2" and "1" templates (see pages 94–95) on a piece of paper. Slide the tracing under the parchment paper.

2. Put the melted dark chocolate in a small pastry bag (see page 9) and snip off just the tip so the chocolate flows in a fine line. Pipe over the outlines of the numbers and then fill in the centers to make solid shapes. Repeat this process with both the milk and white chocolates. Let stand in a cool place for several hours or overnight to set.

3. Slice each chocolate cake in half horizontally and sandwich each with the white chocolate ganache. Place the largest cake on a flat plate and the smaller ones on 6-inch/15-cm and 4-inch/10-cm thin cake boards.

4. Spread a thin layer of dark chocolate ganache around the sides of all three cakes with a palette knife to seal in the crumbs. Chill in the refrigerator for 15 minutes. Stack the medium cake, still on its cake board, on top of the largest cake and then stack the smallest cake, still on its cake board, on top, using dowels to support the upper two tiers (see page 19). Using a palette knife, spread the remaining ganache all over the cakes in an even layer.

5. Carefully peel the paper away from the chocolate numbers and scatter the numbers over the cakes like confetti. Prop some numbers up, particularly on the top, to give height.

HELPFUL HINT
The chocolate numbers can be piped up to a week in advance. Once set, place in layers in an airtight container, still on the paper, and store in a cool place until ready to use.

Music Lover's Birthday Cake

SERVES 26

♦ Preparation time:
30 minutes, plus cooling
♦ Cooking time:
45–50 minutes
♦ Decoration time:
1¼ hours, plus over
48 hours setting

INGREDIENTS

✴ 3½ oz/100 g black
ready-to-use fondant,
see page 15
✴ confectioners' sugar,
for dusting
✴ 2 vanilla layer cakes,
10 inches/25 cm in
diameter, see page 11
✴ ½ cup raspberry or
strawberry preserves
✴ 2 quantities
buttercream, see page 14
✴ 2 lb/900 g white
ready-to-use fondant,
see page 15
✴ ½ quantity royal icing,
see page 15
✴ 4¼ feet/1.3 m black
ribbon, ⅛ inch/3 mm wide
✴ black food coloring

Eye-catching and effective, this simple cake will appeal to anyone with a love of music! You will need to allow at least two days to let the notes on the top of the cake harden.

1. Line a baking sheet with parchment paper. Roll out the black fondant thinly on a surface dusted with confectioners' sugar. Cut out three 2½- x ¼-inch/6-cm x 5-mm sticks and three 1-inch/2.5-cm circles with a round cutter. Using a rolling pin, gently roll the circles to stretch into oval shapes. Using the cutter, cut curved tips off the ends of the sticks. Moisten the cut areas with a damp paintbrush and attach to the ovals to create simple notes. Transfer to the prepared sheet. Cut out three smaller circles, using a ½-inch/1-cm cutter. Place on the sheet and let rest for at least 2 days to harden.

2. Sandwich the cakes together with the preserves and ½ cup of the buttercream and place on a flat plate, preferably black or white. Using a palette knife, spread the top and sides of the cake with the remaining buttercream. Use the white fondant to cover the cake (see page 18). Let stand overnight, until firm, before decorating, if desired.

3. Put the royal icing into a small pastry bag and snip off just the tip (see page 9). Cut the

ribbon into five 10½-inch/26-cm lengths and wrap one length around the middle of the cake, securing the ends with dots of icing from the pastry bag. Attach two more ribbons on each side of the first, leaving spaces between them.

4. Dilute a little black food coloring with a dash of water. Using a fine paintbrush, paint musical notes around the sides of the cake (see Helpful Hint).

5. Carefully peel the paper from the musical notes. Dot the bottom of the notes with a little icing from the pastry bag and secure to the top of the cake. If necessary, support the notes by pushing a toothpick down into the cake behind the sticks until they set in position. Arrange the smaller circles between the notes.

HELPFUL HINT

All you need to successfully paint the notes is a fine paintbrush and a fairly steady hand. For inspiration, get some sheet music to copy.

1

4

5

Dog Lover's Birthday Cake

SERVES 16

◆ Preparation time:
25 minutes, plus cooling
◆ Cooking time:
35–40 minutes
◆ Decoration time:
45 minutes, plus chilling

INGREDIENTS

✹ 2 vanilla layer cakes, 8 inches/20 cm in diameter, see page 11
✹ ⅓ cup raspberry or strawberry preserves
✹ 2 quantities buttercream, see page 14
✹ 3½ oz/100 g white chocolate, chopped
✹ large bowl of multi-colored sugar sprinkles
✹ 1 oz/25 g bright blue ready-to-use fondant, see page 15
✹ confectioners' sugar, for dusting
✹ 20 inches/50 cm bright blue, wired ribbon, about 1½ inches/4 cm wide

No animal lover could resist this gorgeous birthday cake, suitable for any party or small gathering. To display the cake at its best, choose a brightly colored plate or stand and a matching ribbon.

1. Sandwich the cakes together with the preserves and ⅓ cup of the buttercream and place on a flat plate or cake stand. Using a palette knife, spread a thin layer of buttercream over the cake to seal in the crumbs. Chill in the refrigerator for 15 minutes, then spread the remaining buttercream over the cake.

2. Trace the Scottie dog template (see pages 94–95) onto a sheet of paper. Place the tracing under a larger sheet of parchment paper on a baking sheet or cutting board. Melt the chocolate (see page 16). Put in a small pastry bag and snip off just the tip (see page 9). Pipe over the outline of the dog, then slide the template under the paper and pipe more outlines. You will need about nine shapes for the cake (see Helpful Hint). Fill in the centers of the shapes with more chocolate.

3. While the chocolate is still soft, scatter generously with sugar sprinkles and let stand in a cool place or chill in the refrigerator for 30 minutes.

4. Shake off the loose sprinkles from the chocolate. Thinly roll out the blue fondant on a surface lightly dusted with confectioners' sugar and cut out thin strips about 1¼ inches/3 cm long. Moisten the strips with a damp paintbrush and press gently around the dogs' necks. Carefully peel the paper away from the chocolate and gently press the shapes against the sides of the cake. Scatter more sprinkles on the top of the cake and decorate with a large bow, made using the wired ribbon.

HELPFUL HINT
If you make extra Scottie dogs, they make perfect treats for children at a big family party.

2

3

4

Gingerbread Party Cake

SERVES 14–16

✦ Preparation time:
30 minutes, plus cooling
✦ Cooking time:
1¾ hours
✦ Decoration time:
1 hour, plus chilling

INGREDIENTS
✴ 3⅔ cups flour
✴ 2 tsp baking powder
✴ 2 tsp ground ginger
✴ 2¾ cups golden raisins
✴ 1 cup butter, plus extra
for greasing
✴ finely grated rind of
1 orange
✴ 1 cup light corn syrup
✴ ⅔ cup packed light
brown sugar
✴ 4 eggs, beaten

GINGERBREAD FIGURES
✴ 6 tbsp butter, softened
✴ ⅓ cup packed light
brown sugar
✴ 2 egg yolks
✴ ¼ cup light corn syrup
✴ 1⅔ cups all-purpose
flour, plus extra for
dusting
✴ 1 tsp ground ginger

TO DECORATE
✴ 2 quantities
buttercream, see page 14
✴ 2 oz/55 g semisweet
dark chocolate, chopped
✴ 3 oz/85 g each of red,
orange, and green ready-
to-use fondant, see page 15
✴ confectioners' sugar,
for dusting

Kids of all ages will adore this fun cake, great for a birthday or party.

1. Preheat the oven to 325°F/160°C. Grease and line an 8-inch/20-cm round cake pan (see page 7). Sift the flour, baking powder, and ginger into a bowl and stir in the golden raisins. Heat the butter in a saucepan with the orange rind, syrup, and brown sugar until the butter has just melted. Add to the dry ingredients with the eggs and beat with a wooden spoon until combined. Spoon into the prepared pan, smooth the surface, and bake in the preheated oven for 1¼ hours, or until firm to the touch. Let cool in the pan and keep the oven on.

2. Meanwhile, for the gingerbread figures, put all of the ingredients in a food processor and blend to a soft dough. Wrap in plastic wrap and chill for 1 hour.

3. Place the cake on a serving plate. Using a palette knife, spread a thin layer of buttercream over the cake. Chill for 15 minutes, then spread the remaining buttercream over the cake in an even layer.

4. Increase the oven temperature to 350°F/180°C. Line a baking sheet with parchment paper. Thinly roll out the gingerbread dough on a floured surface and cut out gingerbread figures using a 4½-inch/12-cm cutter. Reroll the trimmings and make six figures in total. Place three figures in a row on the prepared baking sheet and bake for 5–6 minutes, until the dough is cooked but not beginning to color. Lift up the paper at the leg ends of the figures and place a cardboard tube (the center of a plastic wrap roll is ideal) under the legs. Return to the oven for another 5–7 minutes, until golden. Let cool, then cook the remaining three figures in the same way.

5. Place the figures around the edge of the cake, pressing them into the buttercream. Melt the chocolate (see page 16). Put in a small pastry bag and snip off just the tip (see page 9).

6. To make streamers, thinly roll out half of the red, orange, and green fondants on a surface lightly dusted with confectioners' sugar and cut into ¼-inch/5-mm-wide strips. Roll the strips around a thin skewer to create curls. Slide the streamers off the skewer and drape around the gingerbread. Cut out party hats from the remaining fondant with a sharp knife or artist's knife and position, attaching with melted chocolate. Pipe features and buttons with more chocolate.

4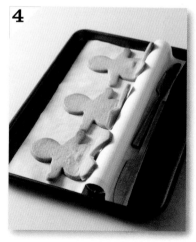

5

6

Balloon Cake

SERVES 12–14

✦ Preparation time:
25 minutes, plus cooling
✦ Cooking time:
30–40 minutes
✦ Decoration time:
1 hour, plus chilling

INGREDIENTS
✳ 2 carrot cakes, see
page 12
✳ 2 quantities cream
cheese frosting,
see page 14
✳ 13 oz/375 g lilac
ready-to-use fondant,
see page 15
✳ 8 oz/225 g each of pink
and green ready-to-use
fondant, see page 15
✳ confectioners' sugar,
for dusting
✳ birthday candles
(as many as needed
for the birthday year)
✳ 1 yard/1 m green
or pink ribbon, ½ inch/
1 cm wide

Easy to make and colorful, this delicious cake is ideal for any child's birthday party.

1. Sandwich the two carrot cakes together with one quarter of the cream cheese frosting. Place the cake on an 11-inch/28-cm round cake board. Using a palette knife, spread a very thin layer of frosting over the top and sides of the cake to seal in the crumbs. Chill in the refrigerator for 15 minutes. Spread a thicker layer of the remaining frosting over the cake, smoothing flat with the knife.

2. Use just over one third of the lilac fondant to cover the cake board (see page 19). Knead the trimmings with the remaining lilac icing. Roll out just under one half of each of the remaining lilac, pink, and green fondants very thinly on a surface lightly dusted with confectioners' sugar. Cut into ¾-inch/2-cm-wide strips, each about 5½ inches/14 cm long. Lay one strip vertically down the side of the cake so the bottom of the strip meets the cake board and the other end rests over the top of the cake. Repeat with all the strips around the sides of the cake, alternating the colors and leaving a slight gap between each strip.

3. Reserving just a little to make the balloon ends, divide the remaining fondants into four pieces each and roll each piece into a ball shape, so you have 12 balls. Pinch each ball slightly on one side to mold into a balloon shape. For the knots, form tiny cone shapes of fondant and mark a cross into the thick ends with a knife. Secure the ends to the balloons, with the crosses facing outward, with a damp paintbrush.

4. Arrange the candles on top of the cake and tuck the balloons around them. Wrap the ribbon around the cake board and secure with a straight pin.

HELPFUL HINT
Cut short lengths of fine ribbon and loop around the "knots" of some of the balloons and stream across the cake.

Lollipop Cake

SERVES 16

✦ **Preparation time:**
25 minutes, plus cooling
✦ **Cooking time:**
35–40 minutes
✦ **Decoration time:**
1 hour, plus overnight setting

INGREDIENTS

✹ 2 orange or lemon layer cakes, 7 inches/ 18 cm square, see page 11
✹ 1 quantity orange or lemon buttercream, see page 14
✹ ⅓ cup orange or lemon curd
✹ 1 lb 9 oz/700 g yellow ready-to-use fondant, see page 15
✹ 5½ oz/150 g orange ready-to-use fondant, see page 15
✹ 24 yellow, orange, clear, and pink hard candies, plus 12 lollipop sticks
✹ 1½ yards/1.5 m each of yellow, red, and green ribbon, each ½ inch/1 cm wide, and 1½ yards/1.5 m of orange ribbon, ¼ inch/ 5 mm wide

Colorful, fun, and so easy to make, this cake is ideal for both boys and girls of all ages.

1. Sandwich the cakes with half of the buttercream and the fruit curd. Place on a 9-inch/23-cm square cake board. Using a palette knife, spread the remaining buttercream over the top and sides of the cake.

2. Use the yellow fondant to cover the cake (see page 18). Use the orange fondant to cover the cake board (see page 19). Let stand overnight, until firm, before decorating, if desired.

3. Preheat the oven to 400°F/200°C. Line two baking sheets with parchment paper. Place the hard candies in six stacks, spaced well apart, on the prepared sheets—each stack should contain two candies of the same color. Rest a lollipop stick against each of the stacks.

4. Transfer one baking sheet of candies to the preheated oven and bake for about 5 minutes, or until the candies have melted just enough to spread around the sticks. Remove from the oven and push any areas of the candies that have lost their round shape back in place with the edge of an oiled knife. Repeat until you have 12 lollipops.

5. Let stand for a few minutes before peeling the paper away and pressing the sticks into the cake. Wrap the yellow ribbon length around the cake board, attaching with a straight pin, and the other ribbons around the cake, letting the ends trail or tying in bows.

HELPFUL HINT
Watch closely when melting the candies in the oven as they will suddenly turn very syrupy and lose their brightness.

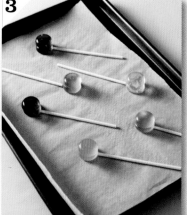

White Rose Wedding Cake

SERVES 28

◆ Preparation time:
1 hour, plus cooling
◆ Cooking time:
1 hour, 20 minutes
◆ Decoration time:
4 hours, plus 24 hours
setting

INGREDIENTS

✹ 2 lb 4 oz/1 kg white ready-to-use fondant, see page 15
✹ confectioners' sugar, for dusting
✹ 1 cup apricot preserves
✹ 2 quantites buttercream, see page 14
✹ 6 almond or vanilla layer cakes, 2 each 8 inches/20 cm, 6 inches/ 15 cm, and 4 inches/10 cm in diameter, see page 11
✹ 4 lb 8 oz/2 kg marzipan
✹ 4 quantities royal icing, see page 15

Making this cake will help you to master the technique of modeling a simple sugar rose. Sugar roses are a little time-consuming so a few evenings shaping them while watching television is definitely the way to do it!

1. To make the roses, take a grape-size piece of white ready-to-use fondant and shape into a cone, pressing the thick end down onto a board or other surface. Pinch in the cone around the bottom to form a "waist." Take a pea-size ball of white fondant and press it into a petal shape, pinching the fondant between your thumb and index finger until paper thin (dust your fingers lightly with confectioners' sugar if the fondant becomes sticky). Curl the petal around the cone to form the rose center. Shape another slightly larger petal and wrap around the first. Continue layering the petals around the center, increasing their size slightly and opening them out as you build up the rose. You'll need 6–8 petals in all. Slice the rose off the cone, about ½ inch/1 cm from the bottom, and place on a baking sheet lined with parchment paper. Make the rest of the roses in the same way, varying the sizes of the cones and petals to make small and large roses until you have 22–25 roses altogether. Let stand to harden, uncovered, for at least 24 hours.

2. Use half of the preserves along with all the buttercream to sandwich each pair of cakes together. Make an apricot glaze with the remaining preserves (see page 18). Place the smallest cake on a thin 4-inch/10-cm cake board, the medium cake on a 6-inch/15-cm board, and the largest cake on a white cake stand. Brush the glaze over the cakes. Cover all the cakes with marzipan (see page 18), using 2 lb 2 oz/950 g for the largest cake, 1 lb 7 oz/650 g for the medium, and 14 oz/ 400 g for the smallest. Let stand overnight, uncovered, until firm.

3. Using dowels, stack the cakes, still on their cake boards, into three tiers, using a little royal icing to hold the cakes in place (see page 19). Using a palette knife, spread the remaining royal icing in an even layer, texturing the surface slightly with the edge of the knife.

4. While the royal icing is still soft, gently press the roses into position so they form a trail that flows down one side of the cake.

Black & White Wedding Cake

SERVES 50

◆ Preparation time:
55 minutes, plus cooling

◆ Cooking time:
4¾ hours

◆ Decoration time:
3½ hours, plus 24 hours
setting

INGREDIENTS

✳ 1 lb 4 oz/550 g
store-bought, ready-to-
use chocolate fondant

✳ confectioners' sugar,
for dusting

✳ 1 lb 4 oz/550 g white
chocolate, chopped

✳ 2 rich chocolate cakes,
9 inches/23 cm and
7 inches/18 cm square,
see page 10

✳ 3 quantities white
chocolate ganache,
see page 16

This chocolate lover's dream wedding cake shows just how versatile and sculptural chocolate can be. Assemble the day before the wedding and store in a cool place.

1. To make the roses, break off small pieces of the chocolate fondant and knead lightly on a surface lightly dusted with confectioners' sugar until soft enough to mold. Use the fondant to make large chocolate roses, following the method on page 76. You will need 25 roses in total. Store in a cool place, covered loosely with plastic wrap, for up to a week.

2. For the large cake collar, melt 12 oz/350 g of the chocolate (see page 16). Cut a rectangle out of cardboard, 9½ inches/24 cm long and ½ inch/ 1 cm deeper than the cake. Line a cutting board with parchment paper and pour the chocolate onto it. Using a palette knife, spread the chocolate out to a rectangle that measures at least 15 x 10½ inches/38 x 26 cm. Create texture with the edge of the palette knife and let set.

3. For the small cake collar, cut another piece of cardboard, 7½ inches/19 cm long and ½ inch/ 1 cm deeper than the cake. Melt the remaining chocolate and line a second cutting board with parchment paper. Spread the chocolate as

above, this time to a rectangle that measures at least 15 x 8¼ inches/38 x 21 cm. Let set.

4. Place the large cake on a flat, square plate and spread with about two-thirds of the ganache. Place the small cake on a thin 7-inch/18-cm cake board and spread with the remaining ganache. Place the small cake on top of the large cake, in the center.

5. To trim the chocolate, rest the large piece of cardboard along one narrow edge of the large set chocolate rectangle to use as a template. Cut around it with an artist's knife or sharp knife, then cut three more rectangles in the same way. Carefully peel the paper away from the chocolate, one rectangle at a time, and rest each against the sides of the cake so the corners meet. Cut out and secure the rectangles for the small cake in the same way.

6. Arrange the chocolate roses so there are nine on the top of the small cake and 16 around the edges of the large cake.

4

5

5

Bow Wedding Cake

SERVES 90

◆ Preparation time:
1 hour, 35 minutes,
plus cooling
◆ Cooking time:
10¼ hours
◆ Decoration time:
3 hours, plus 24 hours
setting

INGREDIENTS
✴ ¾ cup apricot
preserves
✴ 3 rich fruitcakes,
10 inches/25 cm, 8 inches/
20 cm, and 6 inches/15 cm
in diameter, see page 13
✴ 6 lb/2.75 kg marzipan
✴ 5 lb/2.25 kg white
ready-to-use fondant,
see page 15
✴ 2 quantities royal icing,
see page 15
✴ 4 yards/3.5 m white
ribbon, about ½ inch/
1 cm wide
✴ confectioners' sugar,
for dusting

This delicate, stylish cake design is less time-consuming to make than most wedding cakes but looks really stunning. The bow decoration could be replaced by ribbon or fabric bows that match the chosen colors in the wedding decorations, making the cake even easier!

1. Make apricot glaze with the preserves (see page 18). Brush over the cakes and cover with marzipan (see page 18), using 2 lb 10 oz/1.2 kg for the largest cake, 2 lb/900 g for the medium cake, and 1 lb 7 oz/650 g for the smallest cake. Place the largest cake on a 13-inch/33-cm cake board, the medium on a thin 8-inch/20-cm cake board, and the smallest on a thin 6-inch/15-cm cake board. Let set overnight.

2. Reserve 3½ oz/100 g of white fondant. Cover the cakes with the remainder (see page 18), using 2 lb/900 g for the largest cake, 1 lb 9 oz/700 g for the medium cake, and 1 lb 4 oz/550 g for the smallest. Use the fondant trimmings to cover the large cake board (see page 19). Center the large cake on the cake board, then stack the medium cake, still on its cake board, on top of the largest cake and the smallest cake, still on its cake board, on top, using dowels to support the upper two tiers (see page 19). Use a little royal icing to hold the cakes in place. Let stand overnight, until firm, before decorating, if desired.

3. Put a little of the royal icing in a small pastry bag fitted with a writer tip (see page 9). Wrap ribbon around the bottom of each cake, trimming and securing with dots of icing from the pastry bag. Use the remaining royal icing to pipe tiny dots all over the tops and sides of the cakes.

4. For the bow ends, roll out the remaining white fondant thinly on a surface lightly dusted with confectioners' sugar. Cut the fondant into 1½-inch/4-cm-wide strips. Cut two 2-inch/5-cm lengths from the strips and pinch both together at one of the short ends. Lightly dampen the top edge of the bottom cake tier and press the pinched ends onto the cake.

5. For the loops, cut two 3½-inch/9-cm lengths from the strips. Bring the short ends together and pinch. Secure over the bow ends, as above. Cut a ½-inch/1-cm square from the remaining fondant and press gently onto the center of the bow for the knotted area. Wrap the remaining ribbon around the cake board, securing with a straight pin.

3

4

5

Red Velvet Valentine Cake

SERVES 16

◆ Preparation time:
40 minutes, plus cooling
◆ Cooking time:
25 minutes
◆ Decoration time:
1½ hours, plus setting

INGREDIENTS
✹ 2¼ cups self-rising flour
✹ 3 tbsp unsweetened cocoa
✹ ½ tsp baking soda
✹ 1 cup buttermilk
✹ 2 tsp white wine vinegar
✹ 2 tsp vanilla extract
✹ ¾ cup butter, softened, plus extra for greasing
✹ 1 cup packed light brown sugar
✹ 3 eggs
✹ 2 raw beets, finely grated
✹ 2 quantities cream cheese frosting, see page 14
✹ 3½ oz/100 g semisweet dark chocolate, chopped
✹ 1 egg white
✹ 25–30 deep red, edible flowers, such as pansies
✹ superfine sugar, for dusting

The deeper the shades of red flowers you use for this cake, the more elegant it will be. Grated beet not only adds a delicious flavor and moist texture to the cake, but also produces the cake's red color, which is complemented by the colors used in the decorations.

1. Preheat the oven to 350°F/180°C. Grease and line three 8-inch/20-cm round layer cake pans (see page 7). Line a baking sheet with a crumpled sheet of parchment paper. Sift the flour, cocoa, and baking soda into a bowl. Mix together the buttermilk, vinegar, and vanilla in a pitcher.

2. Put the butter and brown sugar in a large mixing bowl and beat with an electric mixer until pale and creamy. Beat in the eggs, one at a time (add a spoonful of the flour mixture if the contents start to separate). Stir in the grated beets.

3. Add the buttermilk mixture slowly to the flour mixture, stirring continuously until combined. Stir in the beet mixture until combined. Divide the batter evenly among the prepared pans and bake in the preheated oven for 25 minutes, or until just firm to the touch. Transfer the cakes to a wire rack to cool.

4. Sandwich the cakes together with one third of the cream cheese frosting and spread the remainder over the top and sides with a palette knife. Use the dark chocolate to make a chocolate collar (see page 17).

5. Beat 1 teaspoon of water with the egg white. To frost the flowers, gently pull a flower from its stem and use your fingers or a paintbrush to coat both sides of each petal with a fine film of egg white. Sprinkle with the superfine sugar, twisting and turning the flower so it's evenly coated. Place on the lined baking sheet and frost the remaining flowers. Let stand for several hours to dry before arranging over the cake.

HELPFUL HINT
If you can't get small, whole flowers, rose petals also look effective. Separate the petals and frost as above.

Valentine Hearts Cake

SERVES 16

◆ Preparation time:
25 minutes, plus cooling
◆ Cooking time:
35–40 minutes
◆ Decoration time:
3½ hours, plus overnight
setting

INGREDIENTS

✹ 3½ oz/100 g deep pink
ready-to-use fondant,
see page 15
✹ 9 oz/250 g deep red
ready-to-use fondant,
see page 15
✹ confectioners' sugar,
for dusting
✹ 2 vanilla or almond
layer cakes, 8 inches/
20 cm in diameter,
see page 11
✹ 1 quantity buttercream,
see page 14
✹ ⅓ cup raspberry
preserves
✹ 1 lb 9 oz/700 g white
ready-to-use fondant,
see page 15
✹ ½ quantity royal icing,
see page 15
✹ 2½ feet/80 cm pink
ribbon, preferably
striped, 1–1¼ inches/
2.5–3 cm wide
✹ 1 yard/1 m pink ribbon,
½ inch/1 cm wide

This pretty cake is easy to assemble as long as you add the hearts in stages. Rushing the decoration will result in the hearts collapsing like a deck of cards!

1. To make the hearts, line a large baking sheet with parchment paper. Thinly roll out the pink fondant and two fifths of the red fondant on a surface lightly dusted with confectioners' sugar. Cut out heart shapes from half of these pink-and-red fondants, using a 1¼-inch/3-cm heart-shape cutter and transfer to the prepared sheet. Cut out larger hearts from the remaining rolled-out fondants, using a 1½-inch/4-cm heart-shape cutter. From each large heart, cut out a smaller heart from the middle, using a ¾-inch/2-cm cutter. Transfer all hearts and centers to the prepared sheet. You will need about 40 heart shapes altogether. Let stand for several hours or overnight, uncovered, to harden.

2. Sandwich the cakes with half of the buttercream and all of the raspberry preserves. Place on an 11-inch/28-cm cake board. Using a palette knife, spread the remaining buttercream over the top and sides of the cake.

3. Cover the cake with the white fondant (see page 18). Cover the cake board with the remaining red fondant (see page 19). Let stand overnight, until firm, before decorating, if desired. Put the royal icing in a small pastry bag and snip off just the tip (see page 9).

4. Take two of the larger hearts from the paper and prop them up on the top of the cake, securing them to the cake and where they lean against each other with dots of icing from the pastry bag. Prop up another two hearts slightly away from the first two and then another two. Let stand for at least an hour to set.

5. Once set, add all of the hearts to the cake, securing them at different angles and adding height to the center of the cake. Do this in a few stages so the hearts have a chance to set.

6. Wrap the wider ribbon around the bottom of the cake, securing with a dot of royal icing. Wrap the narrower ribbon around the cake board, securing with a straight pin.

1

4

5

Trick-or-Treat Bucket

SERVES 16

◆ Preparation time:
30 minutes, plus cooling
◆ Cooking time:
40–50 minutes
◆ Decoration time:
1 hour, plus overnight
setting

INGREDIENTS
✹ 4 orange layer cakes,
6 inches/15 cm in
diameter, see page 11
✹ 1 quantity orange
buttercream, see page 14
✹ 9 tbsp orange curd
✹ 1 lb/450 g orange
ready-to-use fondant, see
page 15
✹ confectioners' sugar,
for dusting
✹ 3 oz/85 g each of white
and black ready-to-use
fondant, see page 15
✹ black food coloring or
black food coloring pen
✹ an assortment of
candies and cookies

Not a cake to go out trick-or-treating with, but it's already packed full of goodies!

1. Sandwich all the cakes together, spreading 2 tablespoons of buttercream and 3 tablespoons of orange curd between each layer. Place the cake on a cutting board and spread the remaining buttercream over the top and sides with a palette knife.

2. Measure around the circumference and depth of the cake with two pieces of string. Roll out the orange fondant on a surface lightly dusted with confectioners' sugar to a rectangle that is slightly longer than the circumference and 1 inch/2.5 cm wider than the depth of the cake. Trim the edges of the fondant so it is the exact length and width of the strings. Roll up the fondant, reserving the trimmings, and position it against the side of the cake. Carefully unroll the fondant around the cake until the ends meet.

3. Trace and cut out the ghost template (see pages 94–95). Thinly roll out the white fondant on a cutting board and cut around the template using a sharp knife or artist's knife. Brush the underside of the shape with a damp paintbrush and attach to the orange fondant. Make and attach another 6–7 ghosts in the same way.

4. Using your fingers, roll out the black fondant to a long, thin log about ½ inch/1 cm thick and 9 inches/23 cm long. Slice off the ends to neaten and dampen the ends with the paintbrush. Secure the ends of the fondant over the top of the bucket, pressing down firmly.

5. Shape a pumpkin using the remaining orange fondant, marking grooves around the sides with the back of a knife. Use black food coloring and a fine paintbrush, or a black food coloring pen, to paint ghost eyes and pumpkin features. Pile the cookies and candies on top of the cake, letting some spill out onto the serving plate.

HELPFUL HINT
For a neat finish, use a fondant smoother to give a flat, smooth look to the orange fondant around the cake.

Haunted House

SERVES 20

♦ Preparation time:
25 minutes, plus cooling

♦ Cooking time:
2 hours

♦ Decoration time:
1½ hours, plus overnight
setting

INGREDIENTS

✳ 1¾ oz/50 g white
ready-to-use fondant,
see page 15

✳ confectioners' sugar,
for dusting

✳ 7 oz/200 g semisweet
dark chocolate, chopped

✳ 1¾ oz/50 g orange
ready-to-use fondant,
see page 15

✳ small bowl of chocolate
sprinkles

✳ 1 rich chocolate cake,
7 inches/18 cm square,
see page 10

✳ 2 quantities dark
chocolate ganache,
see page 16

✳ black food coloring or
black food coloring pen

This is a fun cake to attempt if you're in a creative mood for Halloween! Decorate up to 24 hours before Halloween and store in a cool place.

1. For the moon, roll out the white fondant to a thickness of about ½ inch/1 cm on a surface lightly dusted with confectioners' sugar. Cut out a circle using a 3-inch/7.5-cm cutter. Transfer to a piece of parchment paper and let stand overnight to set.

2. Reserving one square, melt the chocolate (see page 16). Trace and cut out the house, tree, and window templates (see pages 94–95). Slide the house template under a piece of parchment paper and the tree template under another larger piece. Put half of the melted chocolate in a small pastry bag and snip off the tip (see page 9). Pipe an outline around the house template and then around the tree. Slide the tree template under the paper and pipe another six to eight tree outlines, varying their heights (as indicated on the template).

3. Place the remaining melted chocolate in the pastry bag and thickly fill in the centers of the shapes, reserving some chocolate for

decoration. While the chocolate is still soft, create four window shapes from thinly rolled orange fondant by cutting around the window template with a sharp knife or artist's knife. Set aside the trimmings. Position the windows on the house. Scatter the tree branches with chocolate sprinkles. Pipe the remaining chocolate to create window panes and a front door on the house.

4. Place the cake on a cutting board. Swirl the ganache over the top and sides with a palette knife. While still soft, carefully peel the paper from the house and moon shapes and press them gently down into the cake.

5. Use the remaining orange fondant to shape round pumpkin shapes, marking grooves around the sides with the back of a knife, and place around the cake. Use black food coloring and a fine paintbrush, or a black food coloring pen, to paint a bat onto the moon and faces onto the pumpkins. Surround the house with the trees.

Christmas Stars & Berries

SERVES 30

◆ Preparation time:
30 minutes, plus cooling

◆ Cooking time:
3¼–3½ hours

◆ Decoration time:
1½ hours, plus 24 hours
setting

INGREDIENTS

✱ 2 lb/900 g white
ready-to-use fondant, see
page 15

✱ confectioners' sugar,
for dusting

✱ 5 tbsp apricot
preserves

✱ 1 rich fruitcake,
8 inches/20 cm in
diameter, see page 13

✱ 2 lb/900 g marzipan

✱ 2 oz/55 g deep red
ready-to-use fondant,
see page 15

✱ 1 quantity royal icing,
see page 15

✱ red food coloring

✱ small bowl of silver
balls, in two or three sizes

✱ 2½ feet/80 cm red
ribbon, ¾ inch/2 cm wide

✱ 1 yard/1 m white,
red, or silver ribbon,
½ inch/1 cm wide

**Simple, fresh, and modern, this is the perfect
cake design if you don't have a lot of time to ice
and decorate your Christmas cake.**

1. To make the stars, line a baking sheet or
board with parchment paper. Thinly roll out one
sixteenth (about 2 oz/55 g) of the white fondant
on a surface lightly dusted with confectioners'
sugar. Cut out star shapes using small star-
shape cutters, ¾–1½ inches/2–4 cm across.
Transfer to the prepared sheet. There should
be about 14 stars in total. Let stand for several
hours or overnight, uncovered, to harden.

2. Make an apricot glaze with the preserves
(see page 18). Brush over the cake and cover
with the marzipan (see page 18). Let stand to set
overnight. Place on an 11-inch/28-cm cake board.
Reserve one sixth of the remaining white fondant,
and use the remainder to cover the cake (see
page 18), then use the reserved white fondant
to cover the cake board (see page 19). Let stand
overnight, until firm, before decorating, if desired.

3. Cut the red fondant in half and roll with your
fingers into two thin logs, each about ½ inch/
1 cm wide. Slice the logs into ½-inch/1-cm-thick
pieces and roll each piece into the shape of a
small berry. Scatter up to 15 berries over the top
of the cake.

4. Color half of the royal icing with the red
coloring. Put the red and white royal icing
separately into two small pastry bags fitted with
writer tips (see page 9). Use the red icing to pipe
lines around the edges of the stars. Arrange
the stars on top of the cake, propping some up
against the berries and securing in place with
dots of white royal icing.

5. Scatter silver balls over the cake and board,
securing those that roll around with dots of
white royal icing. Wrap the red ribbon around the
bottom of the cake, securing with dots of royal
icing. Wrap the other ribbon around the cake
board, securing with a straight pin.

HELPFUL HINT
A two-quantity batch of royal icing can
be spread over the cake, instead of the
ready-to-use fondant, if you prefer.

Winter Wonderland

◆ Preparation time:
30 minutes, plus cooling

◆ Cooking time:
3¼–3½ hours

◆ Decoration time:
1½ hours, plus 24 hours
setting

INGREDIENTS

❋ 9 oz/250 g white
ready-to-use fondant,
see page 15

❋ confectioners' sugar,
for dusting

❋ 4 tbsp apricot
preserves

❋ 1 rich fruitcake,
8 inches/20 cm in
diameter, see page 13

❋ 2 lb/900 g marzipan

❋ 1 lb 9 oz/700 g pale
blue ready-to-use fondant,
see page 15

❋ 5½ oz/150 g dark blue
ready-to-use fondant, see
page 15

❋ 1 quantity royal icing,
see page 15

❋ 1 yard/1m blue or
white ribbon, ½ inch/
1 cm wide

This simple cake makes such a pretty centerpiece for the Christmas dinner table. It also works equally well using a vanilla yellow cake, sandwiched with buttercream and apricot preserves before icing.

1. To make the trees, line a baking sheet or board with parchment paper. Thinly roll out the white fondant on a surface lightly dusted with confectioners' sugar and cut out tree shapes using small cutters (see Helpful Hint). Transfer to the prepared sheet. You will need about 12 trees altogether. Let stand overnight, uncovered, to harden.

2. Make an apricot glaze with the preserves (see page 18). Brush over the cake and cover with marzipan (see page 18). Let stand to set overnight. Place on an 11-inch/28-cm cake board. Use the pale blue fondant to cover the cake (see page 18). Use the dark blue fondant to cover the cake board (see page 19). Let stand overnight, until firm, before decorating, if desired.

3. Put the royal icing in a pastry bag fitted with a writer tip (see page 9). Use to pipe tiny dots over the trees to resemble snowflakes.

4. Pipe a little royal icing along the bottoms of the trees and secure to the top of the cake, supporting them briefly until you feel they can stand upright. If the trees start to lean over, they can be supported by pushing a toothpick gently into the icing behind them and letting stand until the trees have set before removing.

5. Use more royal icing from the bag to pipe dots over the top of the cake, thinning the dots out toward the top edge of the cake. Pipe additional dots around the bottom of the cake and board. Wrap the ribbon around the cake board, securing with a straight pin.

HELPFUL HINT
This cake looks effective if using two or three tree-shape cutters in slightly different shapes and sizes.

Templates

For shorter trees, fill with chocolate to this line.

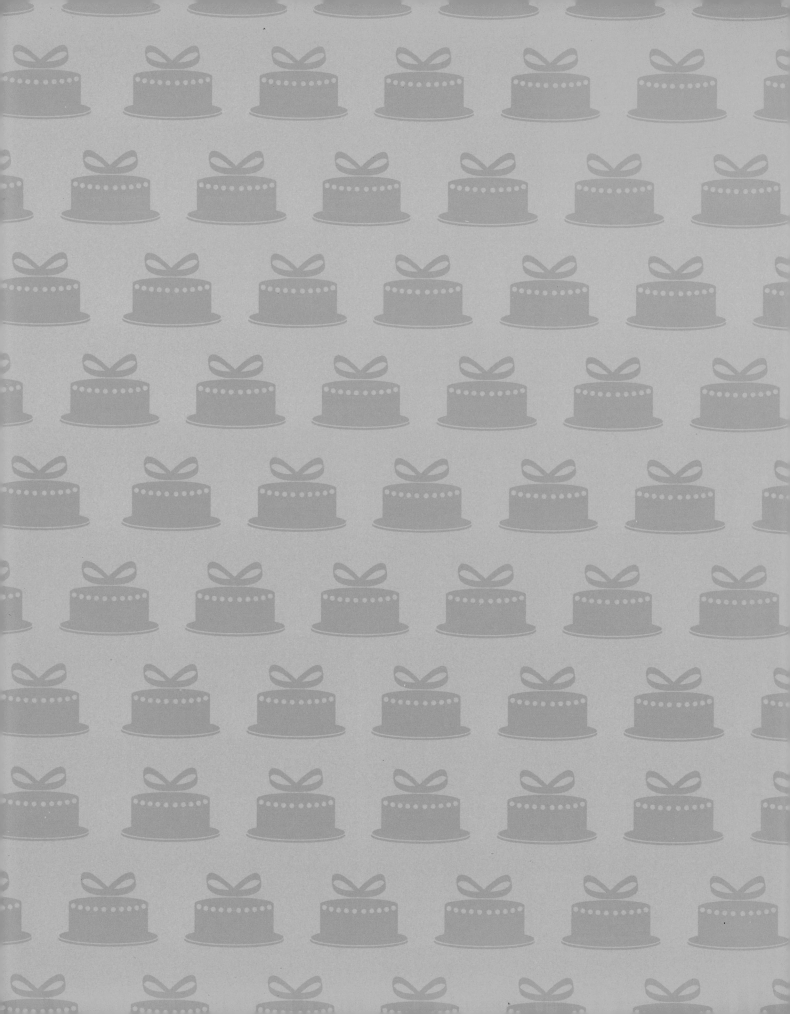